HOW TO PLAY
PAR
FOURS

Peter Smith

Colour Library Books

CLB 3431
Published in 1994 by Colour Library Books
© 1993 Colour Library Books Ltd, Godalming, Surrey
All rights reserved
Printed and bound in Singapore by Kim Hup Lee Printing Co. Pte. Ltd.
ISBN 1-85833-058-0

Contents

Peter Smith

Peter Smith has worked as a writer and marketing consultant for over twenty-five years. He has published books on travel, classical composers and the painter, Constable. He himself enjoys painting, primarily in oils. Widely travelled, he has worked as a journalist in the aviation and travel industries, and was the editor of travel magazines in both London and New York. Peter lives in Madrid, Spain.

Introduction

The majority of holes on a golf course are par-4s, ranging in length from around 300 yards to well over 450.

The short ones are often dog-legs or have blind second shots to well-protected greens. Precision in the middle irons is more important than mere distance.

The longer ones make it terribly difficult for the average golfer to reach the green in two, with only the top professionals being able to hit two accurate long shots in succession. The 17th at St Andrews, the famous Road Hole, is an example and the average golfer stands very little chance of reaching the green in regulation. Another example is the 18th at The Belfry where not only does the tee-shot have to carry the lake, but the second shot is frighteningly long over the lake again to the green.

That hole proved difficult enough for the Ryder Cup stars. For the average golfer, as I discovered myself, the way to play this and many other par-4s is to ignore the par rating and look at the stroke index.

To find out best how to play these par-4 holes, I have travelled to some of the best courses in the world and had advice and guidance from some of the top teaching pros. Not everyone has the time or the opportunity to visit these courses and take lessons from such professionals and this book gives you the chance to share the tuition and guidance that I have been fortunate enough to receive. The advice is aimed at the average player who doesn't have the time to practise for six hours a day but who can't wait for the weekend to be out on the course. It also concentrates on making the game we play a little easier and takes into account the fact that not every shot we hit is perfect.

The advice and encouragement from these professionals, so freely given, has helped me enormously and I know it will help you too.

Hubbelrath, Germany
Marcus Brock, Teaching Professional

10th hole, 366 yards

Marcus Brock is one of seven teaching professionals at Hubbelrath Golf Club, on the outskirts of Dusseldorf, a club that has often hosted the German Open and has been chosen as the venue for that event for 1990, 1991 and 1992.

The par-4 337-metre (366-yard) 10th hole which Marcus chose for us to play is one used as a play-off hole in major tournaments. It was, in fact, on just this hole that Bernard Langer won the German Open in 1986, beating Rodger Davis by a stroke. The hole looks much longer from the tee than it really is, and my first thoughts were that I should never reach the green in two.

The tee-shot can be a long downhill drive, across a ridge some 180 metres (195 yards) off the tee, but the ground then drops away again towards a valley in front of the elevated green. The approach to the green is through trees, though not too tight. My initial idea was to hit a long drive to top the ridge and carry down the other side, running some considerable

---

Hubbelrath

- On a hanging lie try to get your body over the ball more
- Unless you are on a flat surface you have to make slight adjustments to compensate. Learn to understand them
- On the approach, don't be scared of going slightly long

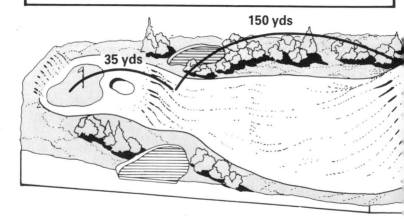

The view from the tee of the 10th hole at Hubbelrath with the ridge in the centre. The hole looks longer from the tee than it really is. The ground drops away the other side of the ridge.

distance to leave an easy pitch up onto the fairly wide green.

Marcus, however, had another suggestion.

"The problem with hitting long off the tee is that you will end up with a shot where the ball is lying downhill, and you have to hit a high shot, pitched up to the elevated green. That is difficult for any player, let alone someone who has a middle or high

The first reaction on this hole might be to hit long off the tee to carry the ridge. However you would then be left with a difficult downhill lie for the next shot.

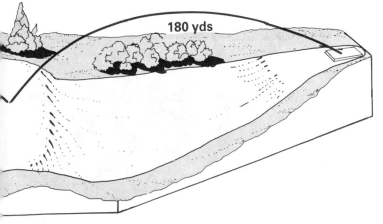

180 yds

handicap. There is a downhill slope which means you would
need to get a highly lofted club in under the ball to get it high
enough onto the green; then, of course, you lose distance. You
would probably end up short of the green, on a steep incline.

"Because your second shot – to the green – needs to be high
and accurate, you really need a level area of fairway to hit it
from. That makes the ridge the best place to land a shot. From
there you will have about 150 metres (162 yards) to the centre
of the green, which could be something like a 5-iron for most

*Playing from a ball-above-
feet position. Grip down
the club slightly and get a
little more over the ball,
flexing your knees so you
are bending over the ball
more than normal.*

players, or a 4-or 5-wood for those who don't hit quite so long."

The ridge, however, looks fairly small from the tee, apparently demanding both considerable distance and accuracy. Marcus discounted that by walking me down to it before we hit the tee-shot. Surprisingly, once you are there, it is a fairly large area so that, if you hit a 3-wood fairly straight, you cannot fail to land the ball in perfect position.

Marcus hit a ball first, using a 5-iron with a little draw which left the ball on the top left-hand side of the ridge, in perfect position for a high shot to the green. I hit a 4-wood and landed in the same place.

My own problem was that the ball was on a side-slope, as the fairway on this ridge drops away fairly sharply right to left. This gave me a ball-above-feet situation – not as bad as one I had encountered at Waterville where it was level with my knees – but just slightly above the ankles when addressed with a 5-iron.

Before I hit it, Marcus told me what he thought I would do.

"Most golfers, in this position, fall back off the ball as they come to hit it, resulting in a push right."

I gripped down a little, remembering some good advice about compensating for the slope by hitting the ball 'up' it. I

The view from the top of the ridge towards the green, a distance of about 150 metres (162 yards). For most players a 5-iron will reach the centre of the green.

aimed very slightly right, but to my dismay still pushed it right.

Fortunately I had Marcus to tell me what I had done wrong, and how not to do it again.

"Most players off this kind of lie," said Marcus patiently, "come back off the ball and will then try to block it, resulting in that push right. Gripping down the club helps, but it is important to get a little more over the ball, flexing your knees so that you are bending over the ball more than normal. Balance on the balls of your feet, and then hit your usual shot.

"If you are coming back off the ball, your hips just cannot turn – they're going backwards rather than turning – and if you don't turn you will always block the ball right."

It really is simple and easy to make the tiny alterations necessary to compensate for not having a totally flat surface to hit off and having made the adjustment I hit my second ball to the green. (We did, however, go down to the valley in front of the green where the first ball had landed, having come back off a tree.)

"On a pitch up to the green, you need to know where the pin is, and then aim to land the ball just past it," Marcus explained. "Too many people try to run the ball up and land short. Never be scared of going long. There's plenty of green to work with here, and no problems behind the green. Don't leave it short!"

We didn't.

Looking back from the green towards the ridge, showing the awkward lie that awaits the player who drives over the ridge without thinking. There are no problems behind the green.

Gleneagles, Scotland
Ian Marchbank, Club Professional

13th hole, 440 yards

In the summer of 1921 the first ever professional match was played between Great Britain and the United States, the home team winning by the comfortable margin of 9–3. On the winning side was James Braid, then a sprightly fifty-one-year-old, who had won the British Open no fewer than five times before the Great War, when the competition included players of the calibre of Vardon and Taylor.

The match was played over a course opened just two years before – the King's Course (named in honour of the Monarch, George V) at the Gleneagles Hotel in Perthshire, Scotland.

Braid had a slight advantage over some of his colleagues as he knew the course rather well. He had, after all, designed it: golf course architecture being just one of his prodigious talents. Although Braid went on to design many other courses throughout the world, he always privately acknowledged that Gleneagles was his masterpiece – perhaps it was partly due to the magnificence of the natural materials he had to work with.

An idiosyncracy of the great man was to 'sign' one hole on each of his courses as being the best. Here at Gleneagles, his

The view from the tee of the 13th hole at Gleneagles. 'Auld Nick' (slightly left of centre) lives up to its name if you land in it. Avoiding it means aiming over the top, slightly right.

The second shot looking towards the green. Once you have carried the first ridge you must then avoid the other bunkers. The sensible choice here is to lay up, leaving a chip to the green.

best course, the hole he chose as the 'best of the best' was the 13th – Braid's Brawest (Braid's Bravest).

The man who introduced me to this tantalizing hole has had an equally distinguished career during which time his teaching talents have been good enough to help his two sons, Billy and Brian, reach the European Tour as regular tour players.

Ian Marchbank came to Gleneagles in 1952, as assistant professional, before moving to Turnberry as professional in

200 yds

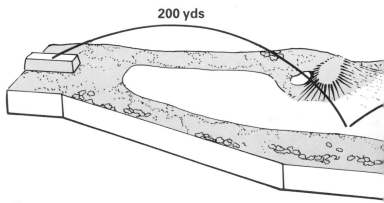

The 440 yard 13th at Gleneagles is probably the best hole on the course with a rolling fairway and some fearsome bunkers. The approach to the green is deceptive.

1958. Four years later he was back at his beloved Gleneagles, and has remained here ever since.

His attitude towards golf – and golfers – reflects the high standards his profession sets itself, and maintains.

"I tell any aspiring professional that this sport, this profession of ours, depends entirely on amateurs. People matter."

The tee on the 13th is elevated some 12 feet above the first part of the fairway, a stretch of Scottish turf leading 187 yards to 'Auld Nick' (the Devil), a large bunker that fully lives up to its name. Avoiding it means aiming over the top but slightly right.

"With the elevated tee," said Ian Marchbank, "you need to hit a good high shot to carry the bunker and land on a downslope the other side. Favour the right side but not too far out, because the rough here devours golf balls."

The width of the fairway above this steep faced bunker is only 22 yards so accuracy off the tee is necessary to equal the test set by Mr Braid.

Failure to carry the bunker should, however, leave you with not too difficult a proposition for the rest of the hole, because there are, as with all well-designed challenges, 'bail-out' areas.

A less than strong player should aim to lay-up well in front of 'Auld Nick', at perhaps 150 yards off the tee. That would give enough room to hit a high shot over the bunker to a safe part of the fairway for a reasonable third shot to the green. One

Gleneagles

- If you're hitting from a downhill lie it will take loft off your club
- When hitting on a downhill lie stand at right angles to the slope, with more weight on your left side

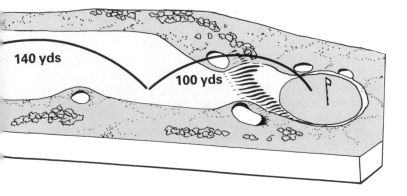

140 yds

100 yds

The approach shot to the green is to an elevated plateau which is well protected by bunkers. Because of the slope of the green you need to aim slightly right of the pin.

hundred and fifty yards off the tee and a similar distance with a 5-iron would put the ball just 148 yards from the centre of the green – another 5-iron perhaps.

Yet obviously the temptation is to go over the bunker. A tee shot of about 220 yards will clear the ridge beyond 'Auld Nick' and land you on a downslope about 220 yards from the green.

"This distance is probably out of reach for most players," Ian told me. "The sensible thing, if you can't carry 'Young Nick' – 'The Devil's Son' – is to lay up with something like a 5-iron, leaving yourself a short iron chip to the elevated green.

"Be careful, however, if you're hitting from that downhill lie on the second shot, because it takes loft off your club. Don't attempt to hit a straight-faced club, like a 1-, 2-, or 3-iron, because you'll never get the ball up high enough.

"When hitting on a downhill lie, stand at right-angles to the slope, with more weight on your left side to support you.

"If you lay-up with that second shot before the up slope which is by 'Young Nick', you'll be left with a fairly easy chip up to the green, with a wedge or 9-iron, depending on the distance. Because of the slope of the green, though, you should always be aiming slightly right of the pin."

Ian's mastery of the art of teaching golf is evident from the way he makes it all seem so simple.

"The most important part of golf takes place before you hit the ball" he said. "About eighty per cent of the faults are in the set-up, seventeen per cent on the backswing and just three per cent on the downswing. That tells you, quite simply, that posture, balance and the way you align your body to the target, are the most important things to work in practice.

"A common problem with amateur golfers is their tendency to try to hit too hard. Relax, always take one club more than you think you need and swing smoothly.

"On the putting green you have to learn 'feel'. Try kneeling down and rolling a ball; that will give you an idea of feel. Then line the putt up, turn your head away and putt."

I asked Ian about the correct width of the feet on a drive as you often see players with their feet splayed far apart and others who almost have their heels touching. Again, the simplicity of the answer was reassuring.

"Nature tells you how far apart to stand," he said, "Stand with your feet together, take one pace in front of you, turn on your heels and you're standing perfectly balanced."

Now why didn't I think of that?

Playing a shot on a downhill lie. Remember that this takes loft off your club. Stand at right angles to the slope, with more weight on your left side to support you.

Seaview, New Jersey, USA

Mike Fingleton, Director of Golf

2nd hole, 432 yards

"The toughest par-4 I ever played in my life," stated Ben Hogan after the 1942 PGA Championship, an event won that year by another legendary figure in the history of golf, Sam Sneed.

He was referring to the 432-yard 2nd hole on the Bay Course at Seaview, a property that, in the 1920s, was one of the high spots of golf on the East coast and that fell into a gentle decline between the wars. Seaview was recently restored to its former glory by its new owners, Marriott Hotels.

The two courses on the estate are in stark contrast. One is a semi-links type course while the other, the Pines, is more of an inland parkland course. Yet they are only separated by the width of a road, making a visit here even more enjoyable – the best of both worlds.

Hogan's least favourite – or perhaps most challenging – hole plays differently almost every day, depending on the time of day and the direction of the wind. From the tee you look down

The tee shot here needs to be carefully placed as there are two bunkers to the right and another to the left further on. The fairway is gently downhill.

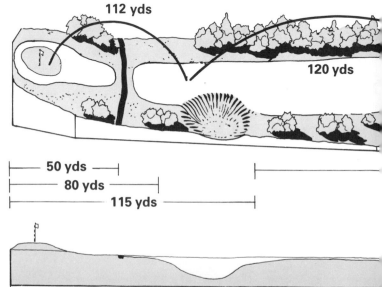

the fairway to the bay with the distant high-rise skyline of Atlantic City, the East Coast 'Las Vegas', rising out of the early morning mist and hazy sun. Although not as barren as a typical Scottish links course, Seaview has that feel about it.

Hogan and his colleagues were playing the hole its full distance. You and I are allowed some leeway, but not much, the medal tee measuring the hole at 415 yards and lady golfers gaining another 15 yards. Its difficulty is highlighted by its stroke index of one: the hardest hole on the course! However, being the hardest hole everyone receives a stroke, some two.

The tee shot needs very careful placing for 120 yards off the men's tee are two bunkers to the right, with another to the left 30 yards further. As the fairway here is gently downhill they look closer in and should present no problem on the drive.

With the average shot being a slight fade, the best shot would be aimed in over that left-hand bunker into the middle of the fairway.

"Use as much club as you can," instructed Mike Fingleton,

Seaview

- With the wind against you, do not swing harder and faster. Swing smoothly
- Plan your shots – don't just hit and hope

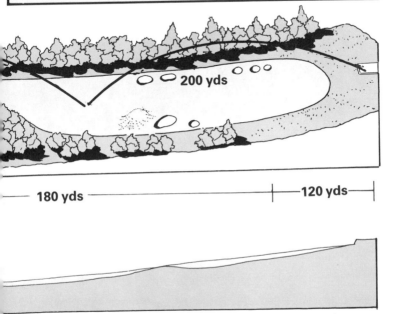

200 yds

— 180 yds ——————— |—120 yds—|

Director of Golf, "preferably the driver if you are comfortable with it."

You do have to remember that the right-hand side is out-of-bounds however.

"Never force it," warned Mike, "because you won't get more distance by trying to hit it harder. When the wind is against them far too many people try to compensate, thinking they have to hit faster and harder. All they do is to mess up their swing rhythm and slice or top the shot. Swing smoothly and ignore the wind."

Wind is certainly a strong factor on this hole, and in the morning, with the tide running in, it is against you. Quite often later in the day it will be at your back and you will be hitting much longer.

My tee shot, with a driver, aimed slightly left with a little fade, came round nicely and sat down in the middle of the fairway about 200 yards off the tee, leaving 215 to go to the green, a distance virtually impossible to hit, being longer than the teed-up drive. Now, from here, with a good fluffy lie I could probably hit a 4-iron about 175 yards and a 4-wood slightly more, putting me to within 40–50 yards out. But Mike Fingleton had special local knowledge.

Mike Fingleton, Director of Golf at Seaview, New Jersey.

"The problem is that there is a cart-path running across the front of the green some 50 yards out, so if you hit as far as you can there is a possibility that your ball will end up on the path."

That would, in this instance, give me a free drop, a point that we'll come back to, but would mean losing distance, so the sensible thing to do, Mike Fingleton pointed out, was to lay-up.

"On the left 30 yards before that path is a deep hollow that you must avoid at all costs," he told me. "Your optimum distance here – as you can't reach the green – is to be just in front of that hollow yet just short of the path, giving you a distance to go of around 140 yards."

For me that is about a 7-iron, but get to know what club you are going to hit that distance. Don't forget it is very slightly downhill and might bounce on and roll on a hard fairway. Here the turf is lush so there will be little extra roll.

From the distance we landed, short of the path, it was just a chip on to the green, which is amazingly tiny, being just 22 yards deep and 27 across, so accuracy is vital. It also had some surprising breaks in it so putts needed very careful reading. We still finished with a five though, good enough for a net par. And that is all we need!

Mike then moved back to take up a point I had raised before I hit the shot from just back of the path. What, I had asked him, would you do if your ball landed on the path?

"Check first that the local rules cover it. Here they do and it is classified as Ground Under Repair, though on many courses it might be an integral part of the course with no relief. You must check carefully and you'll find the local rules on the scorecard.

"As I said, here it's GUR so you can lift and drop without penalty. You have to drop at your nearest point of relief, but not nearer the hole. You can, in effect, go back as far as you like – the two club-lengths do not count here – keeping the ball in a line between your last shot and the hole and then you mark a spot where you have a good lie, but don't lift the ball yet! Mark your point of relief with a tee peg, then pick up the ball, hold it out shoulder high by your side and drop it. If it rolls more than two club lengths from the point you dropped it, you must re-drop it. If the ball rolls too far twice then you place it. It must not be more than two club-lengths from the point you marked for the drop. You also must not clean the ball at this stage – that is only allowed on the green.

"When you are happy the ball is correctly placed, or dropped, pick up the tee pegs and hit the shot."

The key to this hole, apart from the lesson on dropping the ball, is quite clear. Mike Fingleton has the last word.

"Plan your shots – don't just hit and hope!"

St Andrews, Scotland
Peter Tupling

17th hole, 461 yards

The Road Hole at St Andrews is perhaps the most famous par-4 in the world, and justifiably so. Its name derives from the road which runs along the back of the green, and which has trapped innumerable players over the centuries. The main difficulty with the hole, however, is the tee shot, which is blind.

In the late nineteenth century there was a railway – now sadly gone – to St Andrews, running right alongside the infamous 'road' hole. Sidings and an engine shed were built, jutting out into the fairway of the 17th, tempting golfers to either drive over its gable roof, or go the long way round it. The engine shed was pulled down in the 1960s giving golfers a view of the green again, but that was considered 'unfair' by the purists who were accustomed to the tradition of hitting over the shed. To repair the damage, a replacement shed was put up when the Old Course Country Club hotel was built, now in use as a golf teaching school.

The tee shot is as difficult as ever!

Peter Tupling, who spent a decade on the European tour and

The tee shot on this famous hole should be hit as close as possible to the Old Course Hotel. The bunker by the green has ruined many rounds, and calls for a delicate splash shot.

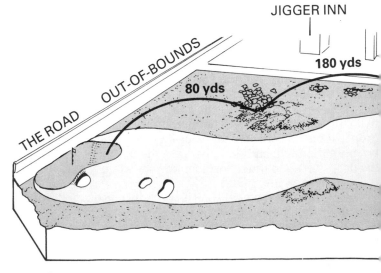

played St Andrews competitively on many occasions, knows the hole well.

"The tee shot has to be hit over the shed, going a little left with some fade on the ball," he told me as we stood on the hallowed ground. Like many players, I tend to slightly slice or fade a ball anyway, so it makes the shot easier with a driver teed at the normal height, or even perhaps a trifle lower as this promotes a fade. A ball teed high is more likely to hook. Don't over-react by teeing it higher to get it to go higher, though; the club will do that on its own. It will only fail to rise if you top it. Don't try to hit it higher.

"Just swing smoothly at it, very slightly opening the face of the club," Peter advised.

The trick, if you know the hole and have played it a few times, is to hit as close as possible to the Old Course Hotel. Don't drop the ball over the boundary stone wall, which costs you an out-of-bounds penalty.

Too far left and you end up in the middle of the second fairway, which you hopefully visited safely a couple of hours

The Old Course

- **Never decide what club you will use, or what shot you will hit, before you have reached the ball and looked at it**
- **Don't look at the areas that you want to miss, but concentrate on where you want to hit**

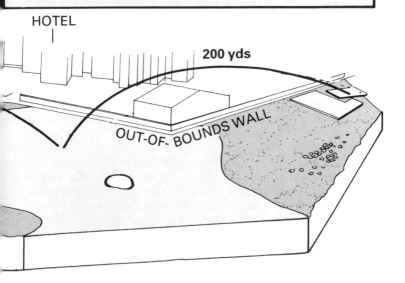

HOTEL

200 yds

OUT-OF- BOUNDS WALL

The view from the tee on the Road Hole, showing the Old Course Hotel on the right. The tee shot should be hit as close as possible to the hotel. Too far left must be avoided.

earlier! A good tee shot should, with some roll, advance you about 200 yards, opposite the hotel but still within the confines of the fairway close to the point where the rough comes in from the left.

From here you still have a shot of about 220 yards or more to the green, a very difficult one for the average golfer. We walked up to it and Peter asked me, some 30 yards or so before we reached the ball, what club I was going to use.

As I still had a long shot, I replied, "A 2-iron."

Peter corrected me.

"*Never* decide what shot you are going to hit, or what club you will use, until you have reached the ball and looked at it.

"How do you know before you reach the ball?" he asked. "Until you reach it, check the distance if you have any markers to use, and examine the lie, there is no way you can make up your mind. Even if you had this shot last week from the 'same' position, you must still only play the shot today. The lie will be slightly different to last week, the pin will be cut in a different position, giving maybe a ten yard difference, the wind will be different. Just because you hit a 2-iron last week, don't make up your mind until you are standing over the ball. Be patient – don't approach the ball with any preconceptions.

"From here," he told me, "a shot to the green will fall short for any but single-figure handicappers. It is longer than your drive. Had you hit farther off the tee you would still have 200 yards to go. A shot that distance, if it reaches the green, could ounce through onto the road. A professional might be able to hit a high long shot and make it bite back, but few club golfers will be able to manage that, partly because they use the surlyn ball and not a balata, which will bite back if hit properly."

In front of the green there is a hollow, but there are two notorious bunkers on the left side of the approach, making the right side slightly safer, from this distance anyway. I mentioned that I thought I should aim right to avoid this danger, being very much aware of the hazards on the left.

"No," Peter emphasized, "don't look at the areas that you want to miss, concentrate on the part of the fairway you want to hit. Looking at the danger areas will help to ensure you hit them, or go so far the other side as to put the ball out-of-bounds."

True enough I pushed the ball out right, not out-of-bounds but onto the little grassy mounds just beyond the famous Jigger Inn , home of caddies and fine ale.

The lie was not too bad – scrubby bits of heather – and the ball was sitting up. Unfortunately, as it was slightly on the wrong side of the mound, it was a ball-below-feet position. There was, however, a view of the green, still some 80 yards away. Peter told me to keep my feet firmly anchored.

"That way you can maintain total balance, which is more important here than a full turn," he reassured me. "With this shot you have to balance perfectly, so just turn from the waist

The famous Jigger Inn, close to the green on the Road Hole, has offered consolation to many famous and less than famous players over the years.

The view from the 17th looking towards the majestic headquarters of the Royal and Ancient Golf Club. Originally there were twenty two holes on the Old Course.

up, trying to get the shoulders round as much as possible without moving the feet."

With the short distance to the green the ball landed safely on the front edge of the green, about 25 feet from the pin. I moved round and took the pin out, laying it off the green, and putted towards the hole. The ball ended four feet short for a tap-in five, which, for you and I, is the only way to play the hole, never as a par-4.

As we walked to the Jigger, Peter pointed out the importance of thinking your way round a golf course.

"Golf is not about being the strongest – it is about being the cleverest! You really have to concentrate on your golf, taking one shot at a time. What percentage of golf is physical, and what percentage mental?"

I ventured a guess of about fifty-fifty,

"But how much time do you spend thinking about your game?" he asked. Most people, he believes, spend too much time concentrating on the physical side of golf, and too little time thinking not just about their immediate but also their subsequent shots. Going direct from tee to green is not always the best way to play this game.

"Concentrate on your golf all the time you are playing," he told me, "and don't try too hard to hit the ball – just relax, swing and let the club do the work. Golf is to be enjoyed, and if you do miss the putt on this hole and take a bogey, so what? Does your life depend on it? Do you stand to lose £10,000 by missing it? If you bogey a hole, forget it. Move onto the next tee and concentrate on the one shot in front of you. Forget how wonderfully or how badly you played this hole last week and don't go round constantly adding up your scores, thinking you only need a par on the next two holes to have your best ever round. Once you lose your concentration on the one thing you are doing – swinging the club on this shot – your play will start to deteriorate.

"Concentrate, but relax and enjoy it."

Playing the ball from a below feet position. Keep your feet firmly anchored for total balance. Turn from the waist up, trying to get the shoulders round as much as possible without moving the feet.

Somerset Hills, New Jersey, USA
Michael Toto, Club Professional

11th hole, 411 yards

In the summer of 1905 eight amateur lady players from the United States, including sisters Margaret and Harriet Curtis, played in the British Women's Championship. Remembering the exhilaration of playing in an international environment, together with the friendships founded on that visit, the sisters set about establishing a regular tournament to 'stimulate friendly rivalry among the women golfers of many lands.'

The first Curtis Cup match was contested at Wentworth in 1932, and they have since been held biannually between the amateur ladies of the United States and Great Britain.

Any golf course chosen to host this prestigious event must be a true test of golf. The 1990 venue was Somerset Hills, in northern New Jersey, a demanding 6,512-yard, par-71 course set in what was once an apple orchard. There are no more testing holes than the 411-yard 11th, a vicious dog-leg that runs up more bogeys than any other on the course. Even Mark Calcavecchia, when setting a sizzling course record of 62 in

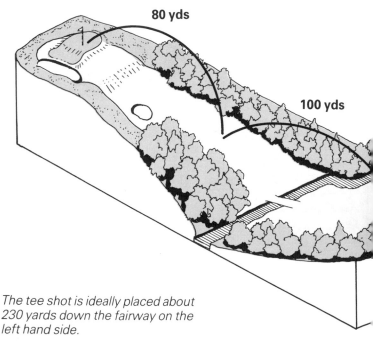

80 yds

100 yds

The tee shot is ideally placed about 230 yards down the fairway on the left hand side.

1989 could only manage a par and had his fair share of luck. Teeing off from the short 12th, he sliced the ball right towards dense undergrowth only to see the ball hit two trees before missing the lake and bouncing down onto the green, ending up six inches from the pin.

The club professional, Michael Toto, who has been at Somerset Hills since 1955, first as a young caddy, then as assistant professional and since 1980 as club professional, boosted my confidence by mentioning that he could only remember two players ever hitting birdies, Calvin Peete and Fuzzy Zoeller.

The hole does have an index rating of two; I thought I might need it. The view from the elevated tee is pleasant enough with no hint of the trouble to come, except that you cannot see the green. All there is in front of you is a wide, gentle downhill fairway, lined by trees on either side, a lake in front of you but way out of reach.

"The tee shot needs to be placed down the left side," Michael told me. "I normally hit a 1-iron to place it about 230 yards out, on the left side of the fairway. The further you go down the better your second shot, but you must stay left."

The trees on the right go all the way down to the dog-leg and

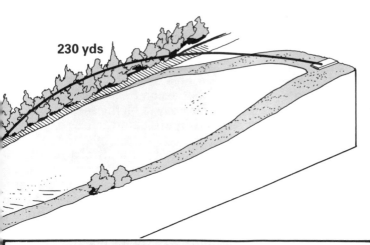

230 yds

Somerset Hills

- Unless you are balanced and have good posture over the ball you won't play good golf
- Think about position rather than distance before you play a shot

If you stray to the right with your drive then this is the price you pay; there is no shot to the green. The only possibility is to chip forward to a safe area and lay up before the stream which crosses the fairway where the hole dog-legs.

there is no way of getting round or over them – you must have a straight shot in for the second.

"If you do hit short, or right," says Michael, "the only thing to do with your second shot is to lay up before the stream which crosses the fairway right on the turn."

Michael hit his 1-iron 230 yards down the left into prime position. My 3-wood was a little shorter at 210 yards and slightly further across, so that second shot becomes blind, though I could see sufficient fairway to hit my second over the stream to a safe section of fairway just before it rises on the run-in to the green.

Michael's position gave him the opportunity of a 180 yard 5-iron high into the right side of the green, though in summer, with the foliage from the trees on both sides almost converging, many high shots to the green are cut out, making it even more difficult. My second shot was laid up with an 8-iron to a position 60 yards out from the two-tier green. From there a gentle wedge got the ball onto the top of the green.

"You must hit right of centre on this green," Michael had told me, "because it slopes down to the left, towards a bunker, a steep hill and the lake. Any shot into the left of the green will just roll off, so even if the pin is cut left you still need to aim for the centre or slightly right."

The greens here at Somerset Hills must rate among the most

difficult in the world, being smaller than average and about as flat as a roller-coaster at Disneyworld! Getting down in two, even when you are on the green, is a major achievement for amateurs and professionals alike, Michael among them.

"While you normally only take one hole at a time," he confessed, "I do often think about this hole when I'm on the 10th, aiming to birdie that in order to allow me the luxury of a bogey on this one. That levels it up."

For us average players a five – which, with the stroke index means a net par – is very good going. Most people card a six or worse. By playing it carefully, thinking about position rather than distance you can, if you master that green, walk to the 12th with a five or six.

"It's a real test of the two most important shots in golf," Michael continued, "the drive and the putt. Unless you can play those two you'll never play good golf. Yet there are no secrets about golf. Pay attention to the basics and it becomes easy to hit good shots.

"The most important aspect is the grip. Get that right and the rest will follow – get it wrong and you'll always be searching. Having an overlapping, interlocking, interweaving or baseball grip makes little difference – just make sure the palms are facing each other and the hands are working together. That is so very important. Get it right and the rest follows.

The view to the green in wintry conditions. The green slopes to the left so you need to hit right of centre. A shot to the left of the green will roll off down a steep slope and may well find the bunker at the foot of the slope.

"The other vital aspects of the game relate to posture and balance. Unless you are balanced and have good posture over the ball you won't play good golf. Be relaxed, not all tight and stiff. To get your position over the ball your arms must hang down loosely, your back straight and your trunk bent over at the hips to allow you to swing through. If you are too upright you can't swing. Get these right and your golf will become like the 11th hole here."

All the holes at Somerset Hills have names and the 11th is called 'Perfection'!

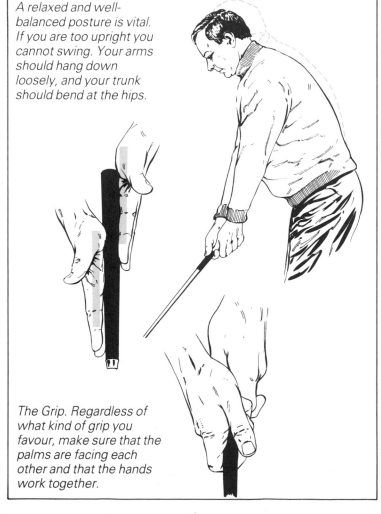

A relaxed and well-balanced posture is vital. If you are too upright you cannot swing. Your arms should hang down loosely, and your trunk should bend at the hips.

The Grip. Regardless of what kind of grip you favour, make sure that the palms are facing each other and that the hands work together.

Toxandria, Holland
Ray Leach, Club Professional

6th hole, 366 yards

The 6th hole at Toxandria, one of Holland's premier courses not far from Breda, near the Belgian border, is one of the most difficult on this championship course. It needs both careful planning and execution. From the back tee the drive needs to be long and straight, avoiding the trees which come in tight on both sides for the first 50 yards or so. The drive has to remain straight or go slightly right if you are to have any chance of going for the green on the second, and however good that tee-shot, the second shot is always blind.

Stray left and you are in the woods; go left and you could be out-of-bounds. The green dips and bumps in all directions, making reading a putt correctly a daunting challenge.

The advice from Ray Leach, an Englishman who has been here several years was, therefore, rather apt.

"Relax."

His advice referred not just to playing this treacherous hole but to the whole game.

"Relaxation is the most important thing in golf," Ray stressed. "If you have built a certain confidence in your swing

The huge incline that crosses the fairway about 80 yards from the green. The third shot can now be a simple chip to the green, but it is wise not to play the shot blind.

Looking back down the fairway from the green, showing how the hole needs careful planning. Hit the corner of the dog-leg and you have to choose between laying-up or going for the green.

you can take away a lot of the fear which, particularly on a hole like this, will creep into your game.

"By relaxing you will retain – or regain – the freedom of movement in your legs and body to be able to swing through the ball correctly. If you are tense and nervous about what might happen to the ball, you will hesitate momentarily and

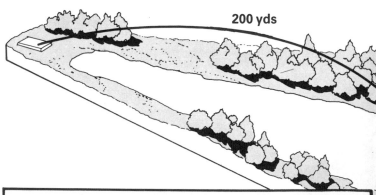

200 yds

Toxandria

- **Relaxing gives you proper freedom of movement, in your arms, trunk and legs**

- **If you try to hit the ball too hard, you are likely to pull the club through in an open position**

almost imperceptibly at the top of the backswing. You will then tighten your grip on the club and quite probably almost strangle it."

Getting rid of the nerves and tension may not be easy but the first step is acknowledging them. Various methods to help us relax have been suggested over the years, from deep breathing and gently rotating the neck, loosening up the muscles physically, to quiet meditation. There are of course those who suggest a quick nip from the hip flask, but taking into account the tensions of the average round, this is not something I would recommend really!

"Physically relaxing your grip on the club is one excellent way of releasing tension," Ray claimed. "By completely slackening off your grip it will show you just how tight you *were* gripping it.

"To hit the ball well, you need good wrist flexibility. Without it your hands won't turn over at impact, but will remain stiff, causing you to slice or shank."

This wrist flexibility was demonstrated by Ray as we set up to hit the tee-shot. I was not getting the club back over at the top of the backswing far enough, but stopping with it pointing almost straight up in the air.

The 6th hole at Toxandria is a difficult dog-leg. To go for the green with your second shot you must go straight or slightly right with the drive from the tee.

160 yds

Trees behind the green on the 6th await the over-hit approach shot, while a sliced approach will be out-of-bounds. The green dips and bumps in all directions.

The power in a shot obviously comes from the length of the backswing, allowing the club-head to gain speed. The further back you can swing it (but not past the horizontal) the faster it will be travelling when it hits the ball, and the more power in the shot. By stopping 'upright' I was robbing myself of a fair distance.

Ray stressed the importance of gripping tightly enough but not too tight.

"Hold on a little more with the left hand, and the 'trigger-finger' of the right, to control the club. Don't let it slip around in your hands but at the same time don't grip so tight that the muscles in your arms become tense. Remember to relax!"

The hole itself is a dog-leg left, with lots of mounds and humps on the corner, and trees coming in tight on the left. The best strategy for the tee-shot, from the members' tee, which makes the hole 337 metres (366 yards), is towards the right hand corner of the dog-leg, a shot of about 200 metres (217 yards). Depending on your length, a driver or 3-wood should be hit straight. With the tendency of most golfers to slightly slice, the ball should come round a little and land in prime position.

For those of us who are shorter off the tee, and don't reach the corner, the next shot cannot be aimed at the green, which is completely blocked out from here. The best option is a 7- or 8-

iron to a position slightly right of centre, just before a huge incline across the fairway 75 metres (80 yards) out from the green.

The third shot can then be a gentle chip to the green, having walked to the top of the incline to look carefully at the green. A well-placed chip from here could still leave you with two putts for a five – an excellent score on this hole where even a six is not a disgrace.

For the player who has hit the corner of the dog-leg, a difficult choice now arises; to go for the green or to lay-up?

"It depends on the lie of the ball and your power and accuracy from 160 metres (173 yards), with a 5- or 4-iron, or even a 5-wood," said Ray.

"If the lie is good and flat – never try it if your ball is in a divot or hollow – a 5-wood could be ideal, but this again depends on your confidence with a 5-wood off the fairway."

A slice, on this approach, could be costly, for the right side of the green is out of bounds, skirting a road. Unless you are confident from this distance, the best option is, of course, to lay up and try to get the approach close to the pin.

Once again, it all comes down to confidence. And confidence, as Ray so rightly says, comes from being 'relaxed'.

To get the distance on your shots you need to cock the wrists at the top of the backswing to allow the club to go back its full distance. By stopping 'upright' you rob yourself of power and therefore of distance.

Las Brisas, Spain
Sebastian Miguel, Club Professional

2nd hole, 397 yards

In the foothills of the Sierra de Ronda, part of the giant mountain range which runs down from the heart of Andalucia, Spain's southern province, to the sparkling waters of the blue Mediterranean is what many people regard as the finest golf course in Spain.

Turning off the coast road by the ultra-chic Puerto Banus, not far from Malaga, the road climbs steadily, past numerous housing developments that have turned this part of Spain into one of the highest priced areas of real estate in Europe, until you suddenly come to Las Brisas, carved, it seems, out of the mountain side.

The course itself was chosen to host the 1989 World Cup and the 1990 Mediterranean Open, which is a curtain raiser to the European season.

Almost any hole would make for a good lesson on golf. The 1st, a tantalizingly easy-looking par-4, has a gloriously wide

---

Las Brisas

- **Faced with a steeply uphill shot, be sure to take an extra club**
- **For extra power, pull down with the left hand to start the downswing**

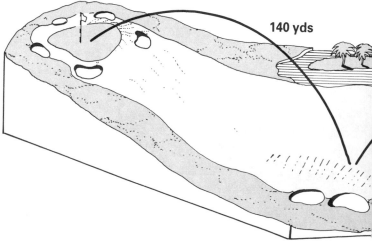

140 yds

The view from the tee of the 2nd hole at Las Brisas. The perfect position for the drive is slightly left before the bunkers. You need as much distance off the tee as possible.

fairway leading gradually downhill, inviting you to crack a wonderful opening drive 250 yards or so, with a good bounce and roll. You can hardly fail to be impressed by your opening shot yet that feeling of 'this is going to be a good round' disappears immediately you reach the ball and catch sight of the green!

The next 150 yards shot is to a green not only well below you but virtually surrounded by water. You have to hit a high shot

The second shot, steeply uphill, is difficult unless you hit the green. Only the left is safe.

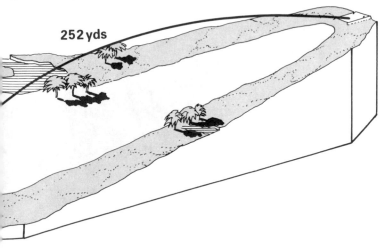

252 yds

off a downhill lie and be accurate to within ten feet on that green. Miss it by an inch and you are already clocking up a double-bogey. Mercifully, my teacher, club professional Sebastian Miguel, walked me straight past it and on to the 2nd.

Again, from the tee, this is not *too* difficult, although the tee-shot needs to be accurate. Most people tend to slice the ball off the elevated tee, rather than staying straight or slightly left. The right is out-of-bounds and, at the driving distance, the entire right side of the fairway is a water hazard.

A look at the plan of the hole, handily illustrated on a board by the side of the tee, showed it to be a 366 metre (397 yards) challenge, with a stroke index of 3, proof that it was not quite as simple as the view from the tee might imply.

Although the shot from the tee, being downhill, will carry, the water hazard on the right comes into play almost every time,

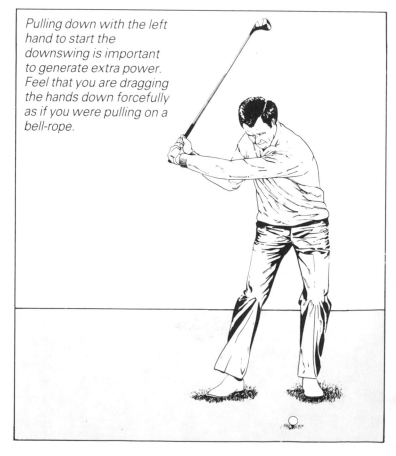

Pulling down with the left hand to start the downswing is important to generate extra power. Feel that you are dragging the hands down forcefully as if you were pulling on a bell-rope.

starting at about 210 metres (228 yards). With the downhill roll, most players reach this easily. The place to aim for is the left, towards the two fairway bunkers which are, in fact, on a side-hill.

"Aim at the bunkers on the left with a little fade," said Sebastian, "and the ball will roll back down to the middle of the fairway. You also want as much distance off the tee as possible, providing you can keep the ball straight or bring it round from the left a little."

He demonstrated how to get extra power on a tee shot – or any other shot for that matter.

"As you reach the top of the backswing you must really pull down with the left hand to start the downswing. The power comes with that pulling down motion."

Sebastian pointed out, however, that this does not happen in isolation, but is driven by the lower body turn. We should have that feeling that we are really dragging the hands down with some force at the start of the downswing. Of course, by the time we reach the ball the clubhead has passed the hands, to hit the ball a split-second before the hands giving that extra power as we begin to roll the wrists.

"When you start the backswing, try to keep the left arm straight so that it extends back well, giving you a good arc. Near the top, break the wrists so that as you get the club to the top of the backswing – never further than horizontal over shoulder – the club is almost balanced on your left thumb. Then pull down

The view back from the green clearly shows the right line to take. The bunkers that you aim for from the tee are on the right and the tee is hidden left.

with the left hand, but you must turn on your pivot. That pivotal turn is vital to long hitting.''

My tee shot, using a 3-wood aiming left, flew well in the warm air. In warm weather the ball actually flies further and, of course, you are warmer and swing smoother. The roll off the side-slope was as predicted and I missed the water (guarded by palm trees) on the right.

Then came the difficult part.

With about 130 metres (141 yards) to go to the green, and with a slight tail-wind, a 7- or 8-iron might be ideal for the distance. Unfortunately, it is all steeply uphill.

Faced with a steep uphill shot like this, you need quite a lot of extra club. Miss the green in the front and your ball will roll back down a seven feet high hill. Miss it right and you have the same problem, Only the left is safe and in reality the only place to put the ball is on the green.

I took a 6-iron, getting some considerable power behind it, pulling down from the top as Sebastian had suggested, and driving it high to get onto the green. But I had tried too hard to avoid the right, and my ball strayed left to nestle in a greenside bunker. So I ended up with a five.

Still. on such a difficult hole, this was quite a good result – a net par with the stroke index. If you can get round this course close to your own handicap you have probably played well enough to win the Open.

It really is that good!

The approach to the green is really uphill. With a shot of just under 150 yards instead of a 7- or 8-iron I took an extra club, a 6-iron to compensate for the lie.

Forest Oaks, Greensboro, North Carolina, USA

John Budwine, PGA Professional

7th hole, 369 yards

Two weeks after the US Masters at Augusta, the PGA Tour moves northwards, to the bustling city of Greensboro, North Carolina. A few miles out of town is the home of a major Tour event, the Greater Greensboro Open, at the Forest Oaks Country Club.

The initial two holes played on the championship course (in actual fact these are usually numbers 10 and 11) are relatively easy for the professional. The 7th, however, a fairly straight-forward par-4, is still a challenge to the average player like you and me, who has 369 yards from the members' tee with which to contend.

John Budwine, the PGA professional at Forest Oaks, explained the strategy of the hole.

"The fairway is very wide on the right where you can go a long way off centre before you hit trouble, yet the left has

Looking up the broad fairway from the tee on the 7th, towards Sissy Ridge. To the left are bunkers and to clear the ridge you need a drive of about 220 yards.

bunkers and a row of small trees before the out-of-bounds fence alongside the road.

"You must, therefore, hit right. I always recommend that you tee up on the same side as any trouble, giving you a larger angle to hit across."

Here, the trouble is all left so, having regard to the large notice sited by the tee stating, categorically, "NO MULLI-GANS," I teed up on the left. In front of us, at about 193 yards, is a double ridge with a valley in between, known to the locals as 'Sissy Ridge' — because you are considered a sissy if you can't clear it! To clear the second ridge you need a carry and roll of about 220 yards. The driver came out, teed well up to get it airborne and with a little fade just to make sure to take it away from the trouble.

I think there must have been a tail-wind because I just made it over Sissy Ridge, to the approval of watching members.

The bunkers left start at 209 yards out, so any hooks may find them. "What should you do," I asked John, "if you do fall foul of them?"

"Make sure the bunker face is not too steep to get out of," he replied, "then if your ball sits up nicely, go in with a 5-iron. The shot would be 150 yards to the front of the green. You would need to play the ball slightly back of centre in your stance, dig yourself well in and keep your feet firmly placed

If your drive clears Sissy Ridge you are left with a shot of about 150 yards to the green, which is a large one, some 40 yards from front to back.

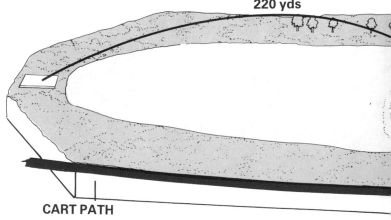

220 yds

CART PATH

with them being wider apart than normal. You would use the shoulders and arms to swing through, and make sure you connect with the ball first. The ball would need to be taken out cleanly, leaving a 'divot' in the sand after it was hit.''

Our second shot – from the fairway, not the bunker – left 147 yards to the front of the green, the pin being another 20 yards on. One common problem for we amateur players is that we don't normally have a caddy to tell us exactly how far the pin is and we tend to underestimate distances. Nor do we know, unless we have played the course before, how large the green is and whether it slopes in any direction.

The green here is very large, some 40 yards front to back, and rises from the front to a 'summit' before falling away again.

From an approach position, particularly if you have gone right, a huge bunker guards the front of the green making it impossible to see the base of the pin and how much green you have to work with. A bunker on the left looks further forward than it actually is, so can be excluded from consideration.

The answer, therefore, is to hit a high shot aimed at the left bunker with some fade, to bring it round at the last minute. This should get the ball starting to turn as it bounces and will

---

Forest Oaks

- **If you are just off the fringe of the green try using an 8-iron and treat it like a putter**

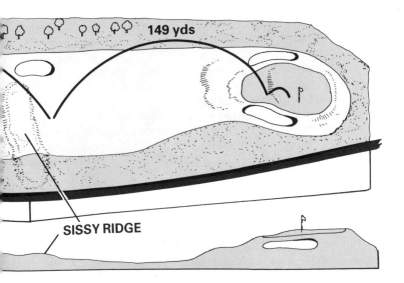

149 yds

SISSY RIDGE

43

The approach shot to the green. It is difficult to see the base of the pin and to gauge distances. The ideal shot is aimed at the left bunker with fade to bring it round.

hopefully bring it in to the uphill front of the green, where it will roll up towards the pin to give you a chance of a par. That is the theory, of course!

Unsure of the position of the flag, I hit my ball slightly short so it hung back and landed just a couple of feet off the fringe.

"From here," John told me, "use an 8-iron and treat it like a putter. Don't even think about a wedge, just keep the ball low and knock it towards the hole with a gentle putting stroke. It's uphill so the ball will bite." It did, giving me a tap-in for four.

As we walked back to the warmth of the club-house on a cold, wet afternoon, John explained that many of us slice the ball because we don't release the club at the right moment.

Now, I had heard this expression before but was not really convinced I fully understood it.

"Many golfers try to drag the club down with the hands to the impact point," John explained, "rather than letting the turn of the lower body pull the arms and club through. This often results in the club head being pulled down in an open position resulting in the inevitable slice.

"What you should be doing is working the hands together so that, as the body turns, it pulls the arms through, and you have the feeling that you are hitting the ball with the palm of the right hand, not the back of the left hand.

"The hands working together here will keep the club-face square as it comes back into the ball, providing you have set up correctly. Now what a lot of people do is to hit through the ball, and on into the follow-through, with the wrists held firm. This means that they stay locked in the address position, the left hand in front of the right.

"But you have to roll them over to get the club-face square on the follow-through. By rolling them I mean that the right hand begins to cross over the left hand, turning the left hand sideways. This is 'releasing the club' and ensures that the club-face is able to turn after impact."

Now this may sound technical, but it is a vitally important aspect of golf. Check your own swing in slow motion; all we are dealing with here is the part of the swing from horizontal on the downswing to horizontal on the way up in the follow-through.

"At the first point," John continued, "which is the horizontal position coming down into the ball, the club-face should be pointing directly in front of you: the blade exactly aligned with the ball-to-target line. As the club comes down into the ball it is

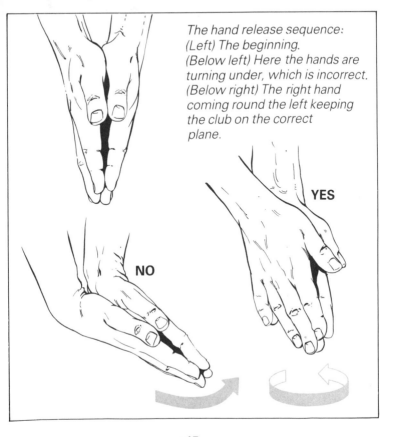

The hand release sequence:
(Left) The beginning.
(Below left) Here the hands are turning under, which is incorrect.
(Below right) The right hand coming round the left keeping the club on the correct plane.

YES

NO

Releasing the hands. The finish. At impact the left wrist has rolled round, the left elbow has begun to bend and the right arm to extend. The right arm adds the power.

square, the face pointing directly at the target; then on the way up into the follow-through it points directly behind you, again being directly aligned on the target line. Use a fairly straight-faced club (4-iron for example) and check it in slow motion.

"As you come through the impact position, and at that split second before you hit the ball, the right hand starts pushing *across* the left hand, pushing the left wrist round. This, like an extra little 'flick' reminiscent of a squash player, adds power to the shot.

"If you keep the hands locked, not allowing the right hand to turn the left wrist, you will come through with the left hand still leading. This keeps the left arm stiff, unable to bend, and hinders body turn towards the target.

"What must happen is that immediately on impact the left wrist rolls round, the left elbow begins to bend and the right arm extends. At impact though, that left arm is fairly straight to hold the direction of the shot. The right arm adds the power."

This is, I hasten to add, for full shots, not delicate little chips or bunker shots where a different type of shot may be needed, nor for shots held low into the wind where the left arm does lead through. We are talking here about normal, full or three-quarter shots where we need power and direction.

Get this right and you won't *need* any mulligans!

La Moye, Jersey
David Melville, Club Professional

7th hole, 385 yards

The west coast of Jersey, the largest of the Channel Islands, is open to the winds and surf roaring in from the Atlantic. On the five-mile long beach of St Ouen, surfers ride the waves while the swimmers lap up the summer sun. High above them, on the cliffs which line the bay, is the golf course which now hosts the Jersey Open, La Moye.

David Melville, the professional, came here in 1969 from Fulford and played on the European and Safari Tours for several seasons. Since coming here he has not only coached a large number of golfers, but has also been busy redesigning some of the holes on this course, an activity which gives him an even better understanding of that vital part of the game — course strategy.

"Understanding how to play a golf course is very important, but is often overlooked by club players. On your home course you will get to know the little things to avoid, and the best places to be in for the second shot. But you do need to think about these *before* you begin playing the hole.

"I was teaching a lady member a short time ago who played excellent golf in the club stableford competitions, but could not reduce her handicap on her individual performance. I played a few holes with her and while her shots were well struck she sometimes hit them to positions that were costing her a couple of strokes. She was then ending up with net double-bogeys on holes that she could have been hitting net pars.

"I asked her what she was thinking of as she went up to the ball. Her reply was that of the average club golfer. She wanted to hit the ball cleanly towards the hole. That is exactly where she, and many golfers, are going wrong. You must plan your way round the golf course. Look for the places that will give you a good shot next and avoid the areas where there is danger if you slightly miss-hit a shot. Make sure your ball is on the best side for an easy approach into the green and take into account which way the green slopes. All of these things are important if you are not only to play good golf, but play a golf course well."

The hole that David chose for our lesson, the par-4 7th, illustrated the point well.

The tee is in a glorious position, 250 feet above the wide sweep of the bay, with the distant shapes of Sark, Helm, and Jethou rising from the sea. The fairway leads directly in from the sea, so a strong wind is a fairly important, and normal factor in playing the hole. In front of the tee is an undulating area of rough which you must carry to reach the first 'portion of the fairway, starting at about 160 yards from the tee.

"You really must carry this distance at least," says David, "to have any chance of a reasonable score on the hole. From the tee all you can see is the rough in front of you, then, at about 150 yards, a ridge that you must carry to get the ball on the fairway. But don't stand on the tee worrying about how far you can hit it. Concentrate on swinging well — something most people do better with a short club than a driver. If you want to prove this to yourself hit an 8-iron, then go to the ball and hit it again with the same club. Now go back to the first position, tee another ball up and hit a drive. You will rarely go past the spot where your second 8-iron shot has landed. If you don't believe me, try it.

"The best side to place this tee shot is to the left, on the flattest piece of fairway at about 230 yards. This then gives you the best approach into the green.

"Go right off the tee and the ball is in trouble, because the approach to the green is totally blocked out, and there is more rough anyway. Too far right and you're on the 6th fairway."

I asked David why the majority of we club golfers so often slice the ball.

"Poor hand action," he replied. "The hands have to roll over as you come through the shot, giving extra power and keeping

The best placement of the tee shot is on the left
where the fairway is flattest. If you go right
then the approach is blocked out.

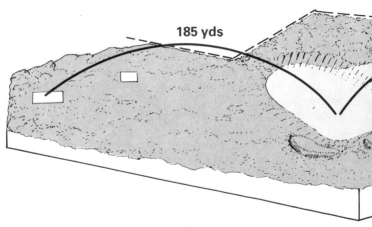

185 yds

The view from the tee on the 7th at La Moye, showing the links characteristics. It is necessary to carry the undulating rough in front of the tee to reach the fairway 140 yards away.

the club-face square at the point of impact with the clubhead path correct. All professionals have excellent hand action, giving them the power and the correct direction. Improving hand action will knock several strokes off an average golfer's round.''

But back to the course. The reason for going left off the tee became evident as we got nearer the green, which now comes into view. From the ideal landing zone for the tee shot there is

La Moye
● **Poor hand action is often the cause of a slice**

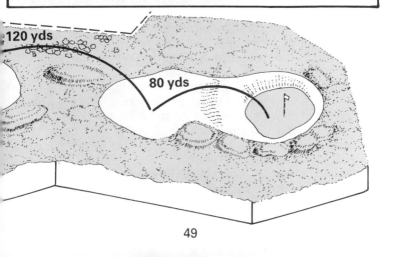

120 yds

80 yds

Looking towards the elevated green from the perfect position of the third shot. A great many players leave their approach shots short of the pin in this situation.

an approach into the green of about 140 yards. The pin was a further 15 yards today.

"Now, you need to go right of the pin," David continued, "as there is a bank on the right that will bring the ball back round. If you hit to the left of the green you are again in trouble; the ball will fall away down a steep slope. The green is elevated so you are hitting up. Hit right of the pin, too."

For a player who is shorter on the drive, and perhaps just makes it over the 150-yard ridge, the second shot is different. With some 200 yards to go, the green is out of reach. The second 'portion' of the fairway comes into play 50 yards from the front of the green, so another 150 yarder is needed, which must be central, again favouring, if anything, the left.

"Here again, however, the average player, perhaps out-hit by an opponent and therefore feeling a bit intimidated, must be looking for the best place to land his shot rather than just trying to hit it to catch up with his opponent.

"The approach shot is, with most club golfers, left short of the pin, particularly from today's position, where the green is elevated and all we can see is the top half of the flag."

This is a problem from which we all suffer and I asked David to explain why, time after time, I am short of the pin on an approach to an elevated green?

"The only reason any player is ever short of the pin is because he either under-clubs, as happens on longer approaches, or under-hits, misjudging the distance to the pin.

In today's situation we are unable to see the bottom half of the flag, our eyes only able to focus on the top half. Our brain now tells us – erroneously – that the hole is closer than it really is and we over-compensate by hitting shorter.

"That is a mistake. We have to build in some compensation and hit longer, Try to go five feet past the flag. Deliberately aim long by a few yards. You'll often still end up just short but be closer than you might otherwise be."

That is a valuable piece of advice as I almost invariably end up short on my approach shots from 80 yards out. I am now aiming to go over the top of the flag by about 10 feet from that distance. And, as David Melville so rightly says, "It works!"

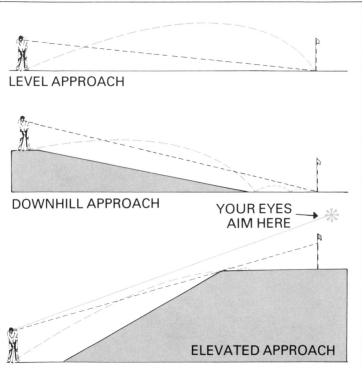

(Top) On a level chip you can see the bottom of the flag and can adjust your shot accordingly. (Centre) On a downhill chip you will pitch shorter because the hole looks closer. The bounce from the extra height will help. (Bottom) Going uphill you can only see the top of the flag and believe it closer than it really is. Most players leave the ball short as a result. To compensate, try to go 10 feet past the flag.

Lahinch, County Clare, Republic of Ireland
Bob McCavery, Club Professional

9th hole, 351 yards

Bob McCavery has spent his life in golf. Leaving school at fifteen he went straight into the world of the club professional, under his father, John. John was at Royal County Down before moving to Lahinch in the west of Ireland, one of the most beautiful and unsung golf courses in the world. He was here for over sixty years before his death in 1987.

Bob took over then, carrying on not only the tradition of teaching golf, but also that of crafting the clubs used on this, and many other great courses. Putters and woods are the speciality, lovingly made by hand.

The course here on the bay is without doubt one of the most spectacular in the world of golf: a natural phenomenon rather than a course built by man and machine. Every hole is a different challenge; every shot needs placing. Lahinch is, quite simply, a course to challenge the thinking golfer in each of us.

We walked out, warmly protected from the March winds, to the 9th hole, a wonderful par-4 measuring 351 yards with a stroke index of eight. It is the glorious high-point of the course, the view from the tee, looking out across the bay as the Atlantic surf comes pounding in, being nothing short of spectacular.

Using, for the occasion, one of Bob's own hand-carved drivers, I stood ready to hit the tee-shot.

"There is an area of rough before you reach the real fairway" Bob told me. "That starts about 160 yards off this tee, so to be

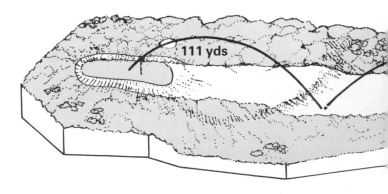

safe and in a good position you need to hit the ball to the left, about 200 yards. Going right off the tee will just block out your approach to the green."

Like all good links courses, it is difficult sometimes to discover which is fairway and which is not. With the rough kept under control by the goats – who also act as the local weather forecasters, as they huddle together in dells or by the club-house in inclement weather – you rarely find a place where you cannot get a club to the ball.

That, though, is not the whole story; it is getting a shot to the green that matters.

"A slice off this tee is dead," Bob told me, "because the ground out there has a lot of gorse bushes, and although the wind may hold it slightly straighter, you would still be left with no shot into the green."

There was another reason for aiming left, apart from the fact that the left side is very wide and open.

"To connect well with a driver, you need to have the ball positioned exactly right," Bob told me. "Too far back and you'll be coming down into it, chopping at the ball, which will probably create either a slice or a wild hook. Too far forward and you are missing the point where the club-face points at

The tee shot needs to be hit left and clear 160 yards of rough. Going right will block off the shot to the green. The green needs to be approached from the left.

Lahinch

- **Ball position is critical if you are using a driver**
- **Let your wrists be more relaxed and flexible on approach shots**

---

240 yds

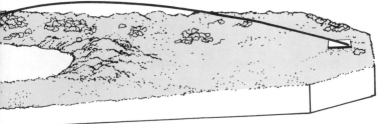

your target. In effect you are then coming across the ball, cutting it out right.''

He pinpointed another reason why average players slice.

''They fail to turn their hips on the backswing. The shoulders must turn as well as the hips, the left knee pointing well behind the ball and, at the top of the backswing, you have your back pointing at the target.

''By failing to turn the hips, even if the shoulders have turned partly, the arms cannot come round enough and the club will be thrown outside the line of the swing. As you come back on the downswing the club is coming out-to-in. That results in a slice because all the club can do is to cut across the ball.''

(Below) The 'slicer's turn', where there is no real body turn at all. (Right) Turning the hips correctly on the backswing with the left knee pointing behind the ball prevents a slice.

NO

YES

The golf swing is often regarded as some secret, technical miracle that only golf pros can understand. Yet when people like Bob McCavery break it down into its simple aspects, it all looks so easy.

Providing you have aimed left and carried the ridge that leads over onto the fairway proper, you will have carried, with the roll, about 240 yards, leaving something like a 7-, 8-, or 9-iron shot depending on the pin position and your own strength.

Down here under the ridge we were sheltered from the wind, which was no longer a factor as we approached the green. But the reason for going left was now very apparent.

"The green is elevated," said Bob, "with a ridge running above it the whole way along the right side. To the left is a deep drop. Any ball coming into the green from the right will just run across the green and disappear down the left side, leaving a very steep uphill chip.

"Also, from the likely distance hit off the tee, a ball on the right will be totally blocked out by another ridge coming in from the right. The green will be out of view. You must approach this green from the left, but always aim slightly right of the flag. That will bring the ball back round, even off the ridge if you go too far over. The slope of the green is also right to left, so hitting right is perfect."

The pin today was fairly near the front so a 9-iron was sufficient to get up, though I left it short.

"Relax the wrists a little more on the approach shots," Bob advised. "Let them be more flexible. Waggle them before you set up, to get them feeling loose, not firm. As you hit you want

If you miss the green on the left you face this difficult and challenging uphill chip shot. Lahinch is a typical links course and fairway and rough can be difficult to distinguish.

Gripping the club on the follow-through for control. Keep the left hand tight on the grip but don't strangle it.

NO

to use the wrists a bit here, because you need to throw the ball up high, turning the right hand over at the point of impact."

It is important to remember that this is for approach shots, not the delicate chips from just off the green where the wrists stay firm.

The swing should feel almost lazy, slow, unforced, yet with the right hand movement you achieve all the power you will want. It is something that I try to practise whenever possible. chipping over bunkers to a green on the practice areas of golf clubs I happen to be visiting.

"Something else worth mentioning about your swing and your grip," Bob told me after I had hit a couple of approach shots, "is that you need to grip tighter with the left hand. That must be clamped on the club tighter than the right.

"You can test it for yourself by seeing how you finish your follow-through. What you are doing is playing the flute with the fingers of your left hand as you finish. Consequently you're losing the grip on the club earlier, and failing to control the shots as you should. Keep that left hand tighter on the grip – don't strangle it but hang on!"

I tried it again. A couple of goats came past just then, bleating their approval and turned away, heading for some sheltered spot. Obviously a storm was coming!

Adriatica Golf Club, Cervia, Italy
Roberto Paris, Professional

7th hole, 350 yards

"To learn to play golf you don't need a golf ball!"

This idea is not as revolutionary as it might sound. It is shared by many professionals around the world, among them Roberto Paris, golf professional at the Adriatica Golf Club at Cervia.

The Adriatic coast of Italy has, until recently, lacked a top-class course, but in 1985 a quality club opened its doors to members, together with a growing number of overseas visitors as the course gains in prestige. Adriatica, now under the leadership of its go-ahead President, Enzo Poni, has some exciting plans for the future, including a further eighteen holes to supplement the present course, together with a nine-hole 'executive' course and a major extension to the practice facilities.

The present course offers golfers the best of both worlds. The front nine are out-and-back in the European style, through pine woods; the back nine offer a circular tour round a pair of salt-water lakes, giving a taste of Florida, with weather to match!

Roberto Paris, Professional at Adriatica Golf Club.

Length pays dividends on the front nine – pin-point accuracy on the back.

Roberto Paris has been playing golf for over thirty years, and still competes regularly on the Italian tour. He brings to his job as club pro a thorough understanding of the psyche of the average golfer, particularly the new player who is a relative novice to the game.

"The biggest problem the new golfer has is that he – or she – just wants to hit the ball. What I have to teach them is that all they need do is swing well – in the right position – and they will hit good golf shots. Without a good swing you simply won't hit a good shot.

"So, the first few lessons are best learnt without the problems of introducing a golf ball.

"First you must learn the grip, the stance and the set-up. Then the turn and swing. That is the important part of golf – turn and swing."

These first few hours without the little round, white object that causes us so much trouble, can also be translated into our first ten minutes or so on reaching a golf course, particularly if we haven't played for a week or so. Loosening up the muscles and getting the grip and swing right are the essentials to playing good golf.

Roberto's teaching methods are successful for he constantly hammers home these points, endeavouring to stop golfers

If you can draw the ball well then the best shot fom the tee is cut left around the trees and round the dog-leg. You could also go straight with a 3-iron.

The tee shot on the 7th at Adriatica. The aiming point is the corner of the fairway, just left of the bunkers. The braver the first shot the greater the likely dividends.

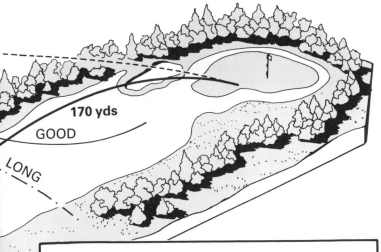

170 yds

GOOD

LONG

Adriatica

- **Forget the ball – concentrate on swinging well**
- **Without a good swing you won't hit a good shot**

Although in theory cutting across the trees from the tee is the most rewarding shot, a less than perfect shot could end up being very costly.

from, as he puts it, 'trying to kill the ball', something of which we are all guilty from time to time!

The 7th is a cunningly created 332-metre (350 yards) dog-leg where the temptation is to cut across the trees to get closer to the green for the second shot. That short cut is an option to the better player, but reaching the green itself is out of the question except for, perhaps, a player of the stature of Nick Faldo.

There is, however, a reward for the player who is willing to take a risk, providing you can hit long. However, the longer off tee you go – if you don't draw the ball – the more trouble you can be in. A look at the layout of the hole shows clearly that the ball hit straight from the tee will, if longer than the corner where the bunkers are, run out of fairway and drop the ball behind some trees, with no clear run in to the green.

Too short and you have the same problem. A slice is dead, so the only option is a straight shot hit towards the bunkers but just short, or a long draw.

"Those are the two options," Roberto said, "depending on how well you are playing. If you go straight you should be hitting a 3-iron off the tee, which will help you control its direction better than a wood, providing you hit it well; your aiming point is at the fairway bunkers. From there you have about 150 metres (160 yards) to the green which is protected by more bunkers, so a good high 5- or 6-iron is the club to use.

"If you can draw the ball well with a wood, probably a 3-wood, you can cut across the trees by a small amount, cutting about 50 metres off the second shot, so leaving an 8-or 9-iron to the green. The better the player the more options he has open to him and the more aggressively he can play."

Certainly, on this hole, attacking the green, by that draw over the trees, will pay dividends, providing your short game is good and you can accurately land an 8-iron near the pin.

From further back, a good 6-iron is still needed, as the approach is narrow, pine trees lining both sides of the fairway.

The braver the first shot, the easier the second. Yet with both options the premium on this hole is accuracy not distance.

Which comes back to Roberto's teaching about the importance of the swing.

"Forget the ball – concentrate on swinging well."

The front of the green on the 7th is very well protected by bunkers. The second shot of 150 yards with a 5- or 6-iron therefore needs to be hit high.

Royal Jersey G.C., Jersey
Tommy Horton, Professional

7th hole, 398 yards

Imagine a warm Spring day, the sun shining out of a clear blue sky after a long, cloudy winter; time to hang up the wet weather gear and put on a sweater and feel the springy turf under your feet. Then imagine a gentle breeze off the sea; gulls soaring above, their distinctive cries mingling with the salty smell to let you know you are by the sea; then add an old castle standing proudly on a rocky promontory jutting out into the sea.

Stand on the tee, 3-wood in hand, and contemplate the huge expanse of fairway in front of you to aim at and the game of golf seems a wonderful thing.

This is how it felt for me the day that I flew across to Jersey in the Channel Islands. The only problem was that, having hit that tee shot a couple of hundred yards without too much difficulty, my second shot soon brought me back down to earth!

Fortunately, I had the immensely experienced Tommy Horton, twice Ryder Cup player and winner of seventeen major tournaments around the world, to help me. Tommy is a Jersey boy who started his professional career here at Royal Jersey as Assistant Professional in 1957 before going out onto the world

The second shot presents a problem for most club golfers because they have a very narrow approach to overcome. The tee shot, however, has splenty of space if the ridges are cleared.

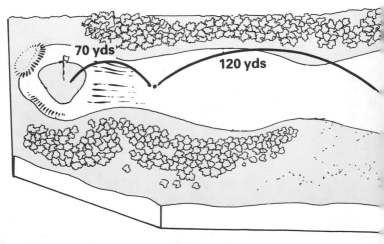

Tommy Horton, who started his career at Royal Jersey.

tours in 1959, coming back home here as Professional in 1975.

The Jersey Golf Club was founded in 1878 on land by Grouville Bay, being awarded its 'Royal' prefix the following year by Queen Victoria. A few years before that, in 1870, in a

Royal Jersey

- If you want to hit left aim the club-face left; if you want to hit right, aim right!
- A 3-wood will help to cure a slice

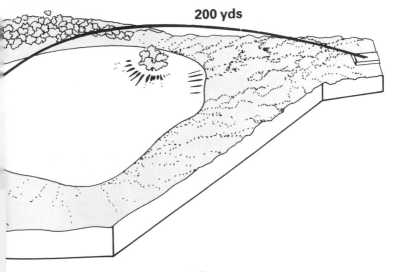

200 yds

cottage that stood on what is now the thirteenth fairway, a baby son was born to a Mr and Mrs Vardon. The boy, Harry, grew to become six-times Open champion, in an era which also had James Braid, J H Taylor and Vardon, the man credited with having given the world a grip on golf, though in truth he did not. He did, however, 'invent' the upright swing and the full follow-through, which gave him such a strong long-iron game.

Tommy Horton is also a strong long-iron player, which he puts down to the fact that he learnt golf on this course. Here many second shots are long and tight and, unusually, a slice into the sea on the first four holes is not out-of-bounds, allowing you onto the beach to play the ball (at low tide, of course).

"The second shot on this hole," Tommy told me as we stood on the tee at the 398-yard 7th, the most difficult hole on the course, "presents a major difficulty for most club golfers, because they have a very narrow approach to overcome.

"As far as the tee shot is concerned, there is so much space, particularly if you stay left, that all you need do is carry the 150 yards or so of ridges to where the fairway begins. However you can go as far left as you choose, even onto the next fairway."

To the right are gorse bushes so any ball sliced is likely to be lost, but I put the point to Tommy that many of us get hung up about aiming the ball left or right deliberately.

"It's really quite simple," he told me. "If you want to hit left, aim the club-face left. To hit right, aim the club-face right."

That might sound like an oversimplification but next time you're on the golf course watch a colleague or two; see where they hit the ball and then check their aim. You might be amazed at how accurate Tommy's explanation really is.

"A 3-wood will help the slicer," he continued, "as he is less likely to slice with a 3-wood than with a driver. The driver puts less upright spin on the ball and more sidespin; a 3-wood, with its more lofted face, increases the vertical spin and decreases the sidespin. And you're just as likely to get the same distance out of a 3-wood as from a driver."

My tee shot, using, like Tommy Horton, a graphite-shafted metal wood, which, having a lower centre of gravity than a 'wood wood' will get the ball up quicker, landed about 220 yards off the tee, staying away from all the trouble on the right.

The green, now 180 yards away, was really just out of accurate reach – an important point to think about as, under normal circumstances, I can hit a 2-iron, or a 5-wood off the fairway to carry 180 yards or so, yet here I was aiming at a very small, uphill green. Distance was not the problem; accuracy

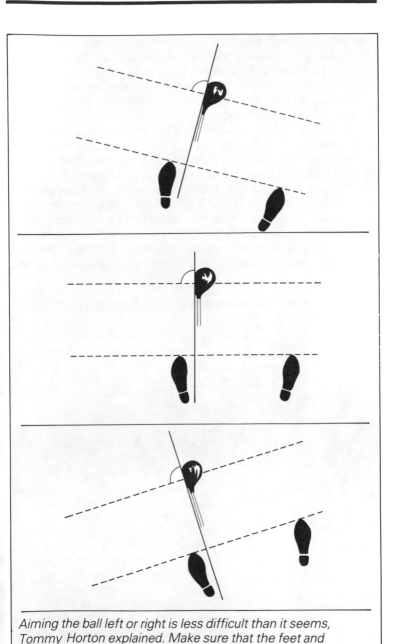

Aiming the ball left or right is less difficult than it seems,
Tommy Horton explained. Make sure that the feet and
clubhead are arranged on parallel lines. At impact the clubhead
must be at right angles to these lines. (Top) Aiming right.
(Centre) Aiming straight. (Bottom) Aiming left.

was. If I missed, the ball was probably lost, thick gorse surrounding the green and lining the approach. Had this been the 18th hole and a do-or-die situation in match play with my opponent already on the green, I might have tried it.

But here, on the 7th, discretion was definitely the better part of valour – so I played safe.

"Most players from here should play safe with a 5- or 6-iron to the widest part of the approach, just leaving themselves with a run-up to the green for a possible five. As this is 'stroke one' on the handicap rating that is more than acceptable."

The second shot needs to carry the thin part of the fairway, where the gorse bushes push in to funnel the ball. The wide part on which to land is about 40 yards across, though, so accuracy rather than distance is the best option on this hole.

"The approach shot leaves two possibilities," Tommy continued. "Either a good pitch up to the flag, or a chip and run.

The tight approach shot to the green. There are two possibilities. A good pitch needs to be long enough to land past the flag. A chip and run could be played with a 6- or 7-iron.

The view from the green with Gory Castle standing proudly on the rocky promontory jutting out into the sea. Thick gorse surrounds the green and lines the approach.

The pitch needs to be long enough to land past the flag – and aim left as the green slopes left to right so will roll right on landing. If it is too long, don't worry because there is a bank behind the green which will bring the ball back down again. Most players leave their approach pitch short because they don't hit it properly. Hit it well and it will carry – providing you have chosen the right club.

"If you're more confident with a chip and run, take a 6- or 7-iron, have the ball back in your stance and stand slightly open. That helps restrict the backswing, which need not be too long, and helps you to be more turned towards the target, giving the arms space to swing through properly."

To learn this it is advisable to take lessons. That way a professional can actually see what you're doing wrong, and show you how to correct it. It is then up to you to change, which will feel uncomfortable for a while. If it doesn't feel uncomfortable you are probably doing it incorrectly!

On this sunny afternoon on this glorious course and in the company of this great golfer, nothing felt uncomfortable. But then I did get a five!

Metropolitan GC, Melbourne, Australia
Trevor Pidmore, Club Professional

9th hole, 435 yards

"Most higher handicappers slice the ball but there's a very simple cure for this," Trevor Pidmore, a professional at the Metropolitan Golf Club and tournament player on the Australian PGA Tour, told me as we stood on the tee of the par-4 9th. The hole itself is a difficult dog-leg which turns very sharply right at the driving distance and fully lives up to the challenge suggested by its index rating of two.

'Instant' cures are something that all of us are both wary of and constantly searching for, and a streak of stubborn optimism in me made me listen attentively. After all, here was a teacher who was good enough a player as well to stand up to the best on tour.

Detecting just a hint of scepticism in my smile, Trevor went right ahead and proved the point by drawing me aside to watch the next fourball play through. He told me to carefully watch their hips on the downswing.

Letting them tee off, we saw three of the four slice, which on

195 yds

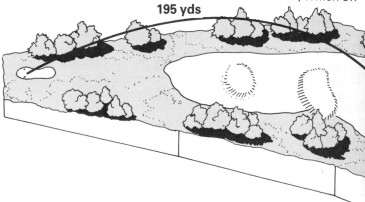

Metropolitan G.C.
- Aim at a definite target rather than just so many yards left or right of something else
- Don't rush your shots. To save time go to your ball and prepare rather than watching your opponent

The view from the tee on the difficult dog-leg 9th at Metropolitan. It is sensible not to aim right but take the safer line to the left.

this hole means trouble. Then, while this was still fresh in my mind, Trevor hit *his* shot. Did I notice any difference?

Well, yes, I had to admit, I did. As the club players swung, their hips slid 'forward' moving in front of the ball at the point

The ridges cause a problem with the tee shot. Unless the shot is cut successfully round them, you are in the trees and dead.

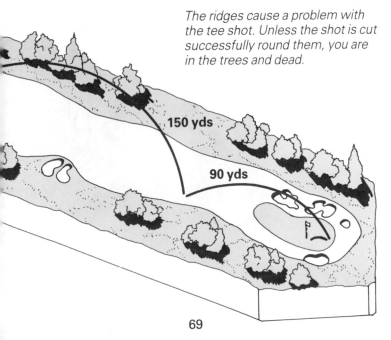

150 yds

90 yds

of impact. As a result their hips were in front of the ball at impact. This was causing the hands to be pulled through earlier, too.

The clubhead was trying to catch up with the hands and body, so the clubface was slightly open as it came through the ball. And what happens when the face is open? A slice!

Trevor then showed me, in slow motion, how his hips had *rotated* rather than slid forward. The body thus pivots rather than moves, bringing the hands back to the address position – which is the only time we're in perfect shape, or should be if we align properly.

"It's like swinging standing in a box," Trevor continued. "You can twist and turn inside that box but you can't move your lower body out of it. Your arms move, of course, but as they're attached to your body they just go in an arc.

'By keeping your hips static relative to the ball position, but *turning* them into the ball, you maintain your balance and return the club to the set-up position.

"Also, you are not dragging the club through the ball" – remember this is for long shots including the tee shot, not for

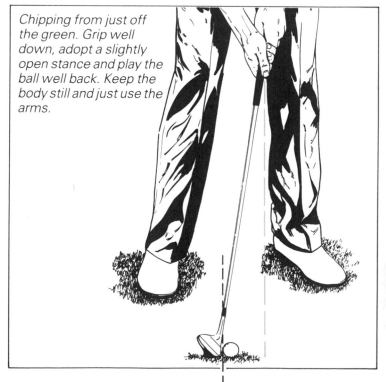

Chipping from just off the green. Grip well down, adopt a slightly open stance and play the ball well back. Keep the body still and just use the arms.

delicate little chip shots where your body starts in a different position anyway – "but swinging through it, letting the clubhead hit the ball before your hands. On a tee shot the club must come through first, swinging through with its own momentum. The hands follow it.

"That way you get the full loft of the club, the power and the right direction."

When you try it you can actually feel the difference. The clubhead comes through faster and your balance feels more stable. Providing you work on training your body and mind to do this, giving you the feeling that your hips are not moving out of position but just twisting, and that the clubhead is hitting the ball before your hands come through, you will be able to take advantage of a cure that is as 'instant' as any I have found.

Having satisfactorily overcome the 'sliding hips' problem, I teed off. The prominent feature on the tee shot is the pair of mounds on the right corner of the dog-leg. To carry them both you need a carry of something like 228 yards. The temptation is to go round them to the left, but this inevitably lengthens the hole, and there is the possibility that you run out of fairway on the left.

"With a very good player who can carry a ball 220 yards with fade, the best shot would be straight at the mounds, hoping to cut it round them," Trevor told me. "If you miss you're in the trees and dead!" I took a 3-wood and aimed left.

The second shot to the green of about 200 yards. The left of the green is well bunkered, so hitting towards the right is safest. The professional's shop makes a good aiming point.

The ball landed on the tip of the fairway in the corner – another yard and I would have been in the rough. The distance left to the front of the green was 210 yards.

"Hitting towards the right is safest here," Trevor advised. "The left of the green is well bunkered and on the right there are a few mounds that will help pull the ball back in on course. Aim slightly right of the green, straight at the pro shop which we can see in the distance."

Aiming at a *definite* target is something every better player will always do, rather than just aiming so many yards left or right of something else. Always choose a landmark!

On the couch (pronounced 'kooch') grass in Australia the ball is always sitting up and it tends to come off clean. I don't normally take much divot on my shots – none of my teachers has so far tried to change this, nor commented adversely on it incidentally – and here in Australia I was taking the ball off with hardly a mark on the fairway, even finding it possible to hit a driver off the fairway for extra distance on par-5s when the target was not too tight. This type of grass does, however, slow the ball down once it hits so you get very little roll, unlike, for example, the firm fairways of a links course in Scotland where the ball will run a long way.

A 4-iron here got the ball almost to the fringe, just off the green at the right front, those mounds having done their work properly. We had 45 yards to the pin, which was on the back, upper tier of this two-tier green.

"To get the ball to run up use a 9-iron with the ball back in your stance and hands pressed forward, and chip it onto the green," Trevor told me. "Too many people miss chip shots because they fail to get the ball airborne. They try to almost run

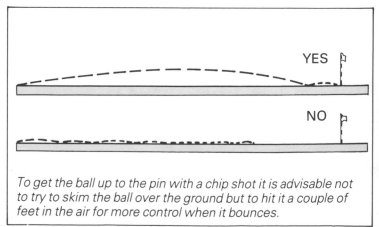

To get the ball up to the pin with a chip shot it is advisable not to try to skim the ball over the ground but to hit it a couple of feet in the air for more control when it bounces.

My shot here is just off the green on the fringe and I am planning a pitch and run. Trevor recommends choosing a precise spot where you want your ball to land.

it along, particularly from off the green, rather than getting it *off* the ground – not high like a pitch shot, but a couple of feet off the ground, depending on the distance. You must get it up; don't skim it along. That way you control it once it bounces – it bites and then rolls gently on."

I ended a little long, but putted back in for a five, net four.

"Don't rush your shots," was Trevor's comment when I asked him how the average player could improve his golf. "Take an extra few seconds thinking about your shots *before* you hit them rather than five minutes looking for the ball afterwards! While you don't want to play slow golf you must not hurry your shots. If you want to save time go to your ball and get prepared rather than spending time watching your opponent. When he is playing be thinking about your own shot.

"Also, don't let players behind pressure you into rushing your shots. They will take just as long as you to complete a hole, unless you're in the trees looking for your ball. By the same token don't put pressure on players in front of you. Don't hang about on the greens – too many players mark their putts and play in strict rotation. If your opponent is not ready and does not object, play your own shot. But take a few extra seconds on your own shots. That way you'll end up playing fewer shots on each round."

Drottningholm, Sweden
Charlotte Montgomery, Professional

13th hole, 363 yards

Around the bustling city of Stockholm are many islands – 'holm' being the Swedish for island. 'Queen's Island', is the golf course of the same name – Drottningholm.

The course was opened in 1959 by King Gustav VI Adolf, a keen golfer, who often used to drive across the park from the Royal Family's summer residence, a glorious mix of seventeenth century French and English architecture. The royal park adjoins the golf course. Today Drottningholm hosts the Scandinavian Enterprise Open as well as several other European men's or ladies' events.

It is, then, perhaps fitting that the main teaching professional at the club is a lady – Charlotte Montgomery. Very early one Spring morning, the dew still heavy on the fairways, we went out to the 13th hole on this testing course; a hole known locally as the 'Oak Hole' due to the large tree which stands guard over the middle of the first part of the fairway. In point of fact the tree

The large lime tree that stands guard over the middle of the first part of the fairway 100 yards from the tee is clearly visible.

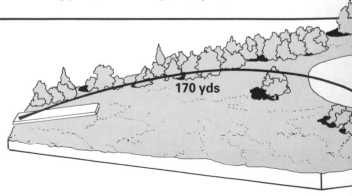

Drottningholm
- **Visualize the type of shot you want to hit – high, low, draw, fade**
- **Concentrate on the *positive***
- **Never hit without a definite aim in mind**
- **On a long putt, aim for a specific point close to the hole**

170 yds

is not an oak at all, but a Linde tree (lime). 'The Oak Hole' seems to roll off the tongue much better, however.

Charlotte's first comment was that, if she ever designed a golf course, there wouldn't *be* a thirteenth hole.

"Airplanes miss out the thirteenth row, and most hotels skip from the twelfth floor to the fourteenth. I don't see why golf courses should be any different!"

I wondered where that would leave the nineteenth?

The 13th measures 335 metres (363 yards) from the championship tee, club players gaining 25 metres under normal circumstances, though we played from between them at 320 metres (347 yards). With an index of twelve, most of us gain a stroke.

Looking at the hole from the tee, the Linde tree dominates the centre right of the opening to the fairway. On the left a line of trees narrows the aiming line; it is essential to hug this line in order to avoid the large tree. A slight fade is ideal.

"What are your first thoughts on reaching the tee?" Charlotte asked me. "When you reach the tee it is often a good idea to step back a few paces and survey the scene, looking from the point where the ball will be teed to the point where you want it.

"Visualize the type of shot you want — high, low, fade, draw. Really concentrate on getting a vivid picture in your mind of exactly what you want to do, not just where you want to aim.

"Don't specifically look for any trouble, but if you know there is a difficulty on the hole — like the tree here — be aware of it but then think of how you want to avoid it. If you concentrate on the hazard it will draw you like a magnet, but if you concentrate on the good shot, that can help you too.

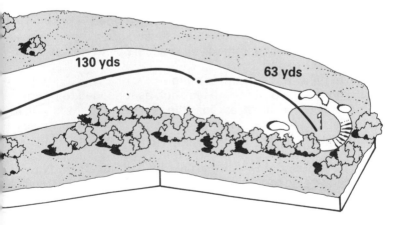

Improving your alignment. Select a mark on the ground some three feet from the ball. Set up the club on that line from the side but about half-way behind the ball so that your eyes are close to the line.

"Concentrate on the *positive*! Then move forward, choose the club you feel will best do the job – not necessarily the driver on every hole – and get ready to hit the shot."

Charlotte explained that at varying stages of the golf shot we have different aims.

"When you have a few practice swings, your aim is to feel good and loose. If you hit some balls on the practice range your aim is to hit some good shots. On the tee your aim is something different – to hit the ball to a specific target. Those aims are increasingly difficult, but you need to feel good – positive – about all of them. Swinging without feeling good is pointless – so is trying to hit a shot unless you can feel positive about what you are *trying* to do.

"Never hit without an aim in mind."

We chose a 3-wood for the tee shot, as it needed to be kept under control as much as possible, yet distance was not a major factor. A good feeling, some practice swings, very careful alignment and then a smooth swing sent the ball flying away from the tee.

It travelled straight, with hardly any fade or draw. Now I mentioned going round the tree. The other way, which I frankly would not recommend to anyone, is to go straight through it, which is exactly what I did. Fortunately the branches and leaves only took a little sting out of the shot without deflecting it. Thirteen is obviously lucky for some of us!

Charlotte improved my alignment for my next shot.

"You often see professionals approach the ball from behind, lining the shot up and then picking some mark on the ground within three feet of the ball as their guide. It can be a daisy, a twig, a divot or anything else. There are always marks on the tee and on the fairway.

"But then set the club on that line from very close to the ball, roughly half behind it but on the side, so that your eyes are close to the line. Once you are happy with that, then step back to the address position.

"By the time you address the ball, you should have made all your decisions about the shot. Don't change anything at this point, unless you have a bad feeling about it. If you do, start the whole set-up procedure all over again.

"The idea is not to rush the shots too much – but don't take six hours to play a round. Once you are by the ball, give yourself a few seconds to think about the shot rather than just blasting away at it without thinking what you are trying to do."

The ball had landed well, in the right side of the fairway 15 metres short of the 150 metre (163 yards) marker; the tree had

On the green it is a good idea to have a specific target on the side that you want but make it right by the hole. Keep that spot in mind and then aim for it.

slowed it down, taking distance off the shot. With 165 metres (179 yards) to go, into the wind and slightly uphill, it was decision time. Do you go for the green or lay it up safely? A slight mis-hit and the shot for the green could land in trouble or, more likely, still short. We chose the lay-up.

An 8-iron sent my ball to the fat part of the fairway 60 metres (65 yards) short of the pin, from where a pitching wedge to just past the flag had it on the green for three.

Once on the green the putt had a slight left-to-right break and was downhill, though the green, still soaked in early morning dew, was slower than it would be later in the day.

"Once you have read the putt," Charlotte said, "aim for a specific target on the side you want, but make it right up by the hole. Then keep that spot in mind and aim for it.

"On a fast putt, especially downhill, you can slow the ball down by hitting it thin!"

The first putt slid eighteen inches past the pin, leaving a straight putt back up hill to the hole. Here again, Charlotte made the point about concentrating on a specific point in the back of the hole.

"Look at the *back* of the hole – not the front!"

As we walked back to the club-house in the early morning sun for coffee – and breakfast – Charlotte emphasized how important it is to have an aiming point even on long shots where the target is in the far distance. Preferably choose one in the air rather than on the ground. That way, your mind immediately concentrates on getting the ball up in the air.

"It comes back to having good, confident thoughts about the way the shot will turn out. Think good – you'll play good!"

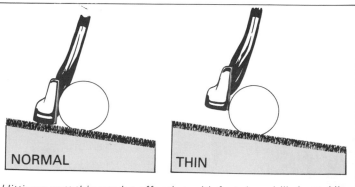

NORMAL   THIN

Hitting a putt thin can be effective with fast downhill shots. Hit only the top half of the ball rather than the centre. It is quite like topping the ball.

Tanglewood, N. Carolina, USA
Linwood Taylor, Head Professional

3rd hole, 421 yards

'A golfing masterpiece' is how the guide books describe Tanglewood, two beautiful courses designed by Robert Trent Jones in 1957 in the grounds of Tanglewood Park, a vast 1,150 acre estate that originally belonged to the R J Reynolds family, but which has now passed into public ownership.

The park not only hosts golf but also riding, camping, fishing, swimming, tennis, a miniature railway, polo and outdoor summer music concerts given by the Winston-Salem Symphony Orchestra. It is also the home of the Vantage Classic, the richest event on the Senior PGA Tour, an event won in 1989 by Gary Player.

The head professional at Tanglewood, which, unlike most of the other courses we have visited, is a public course with no membership (putting it in the same category as St Andrews), is Linwood Taylor, a professional whose teaching methods and golfing skills both on and off the course are among the most respected in America.

Linwood chose for our lesson the most difficult par-4 on the championship course, the 421-yard 3rd. Although the 'championship' tee is further back, at 444 yards, the Seniors play it from the middle-back tees, just like you and I.

The view from the tee on the 3rd hole at Tanglewood showing the magnificent parkland scenery. The course was designed by Robert Trent Jones and is now in public ownership.

"The major problem on the tee-shot," Linwood began, "is the way the fairway slopes right-to-left at the driving distance, where there is a bunker on the right. Thus, if you try to hit left and avoid it you'll find your ball rolling down towards the trees and into the rough."

It was, he pointed out, better to lay up in front of the bunker which, from our tee is 209 yards out, staying right, almost in line with it.

"That way you have a clear second shot although you won't reach the green."

He suggested a 3-wood with some fade, aiming it to come round towards the bunker. In summer the trees extend out into the fairway so that a fade is necessary, starting the ball off down the middle of the fairway and cutting it round. That, of course, loses distance but if you run the ball too far, you will be faced with a fairway bunker shot for the second.

This hole collects more bogeys off the Seniors than any other on the course and rates an index of three, giving virtually everybody an extra stroke. To play good golf you really must play the hole, therefore, or any other hole with such a difficulty

Tanglewood

- Always look at a hole's stroke index, not just at the par-rating
- Try spending half an hour or more practising before you go onto the course

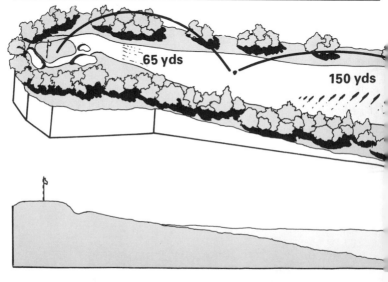

65 yds

150 yds

rating, as a par-5. Unless feeling in either a very optimistic or very fatalistic mood, play it as a five, using that extra stroke to record a net par.

Too many of us, if we are honest, just look at the par-rating on a hole, not its *stroke index*. But what is the point of having a handicap if we don't use it?

From our landing point just short of that bunker, the second shot is also a lay-up, this time just in front of the terribly difficult bunkered green.

"You have about 215 yards to the centre of the green," Linwood reminded me. "That distance is almost impossible for the average golfer – your drive is about that distance off a tee – and there is little hope of getting the ball up high enough to land softly on the green. If you hit it low you'll catch the sand traps in front of the green.

"Hit about 150 yards, to lay-up some 60–70 yards out, giving yourself the chance to get a wedge under the ball to get up to the green with some degree of precision in the placement."

A 6-iron did the trick – enough to get 150 yards but not enough to reach the danger immediately in front of the green – landing slightly left again as the fairway still slopes right to left. We were left with just about 65 yards to go, from which a wedge placed the ball close enough for two putts for a net par,

The tee shot is the main difficulty. If you hit left to avoid the bunker you run the risk of the ball rolling down the right-to-left slope and into the rough. The sensible way to play the hole is to use the stroke that the average handicapper receives.

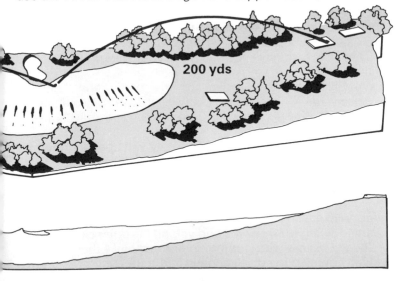

The view back down the fairway from the green. Players who try to reach the green with their 2nd shot may well end up in the bunkers at the front of the green.

exactly as Linwood had suggested. Trying to play it as a par-4 would probably have overstrained the tee shot, either catching the bunker or worse; the second could well have caught the traps in front of the green, and we could easily have ended with a six or seven. Playing it sensibly, and within our capabilities – an easy 3-wood, a 6-iron and a wedge – made it relatively easy to card a five.

"The place you make it up on this hole, and on many others," Linwood continued, "is in the short game. Hence, for example, the pin can be cut in a very difficult position on the rear left, guarded by a bunker which extends out into the line of flight. The green is saucer shaped so even when you get to the green it is not all over, unless you can place your wedge shot in close to the pin."

We discussed this aspect of the game and Linwood expressed the belief shared, I know, by many professionals the world over, that not enough time is spent on practising the short game.

"If you watch people practising they will spend eighty per cent of their time hitting the driver or long shots. Then, to finish with, they might hit a few 7-irons.

"What they ought to be doing is spending eighty per cent of their time hitting 9-irons until they can hit perfectly placed shots with it every time. Then move out into the longer clubs. Learn to swing a 9-iron well and you hit the other clubs well.

"It is the same with putting. Everyone thinks they can putt, yet how many putts do they need in a round of golf? It should be 36. That, in theory, is about fifty per cent of the game – does it get fifty per cent of your practice time?"

Linwood had another useful suggestion for practising.

"I strongly urge everyone to spend half an hour or more practising before they play, and then take onto the course what they have been doing on the practice ground. If, for example, you have been hitting fade after fade on the practice area, don't get on the first tee and expect to hit a draw. Use the knowledge that you are likely to hit a fade, as you have been doing for a half-hour, aim left and work the ball round."

Tanglewood, while being a public course, has a thriving junior section where youngsters can learn the game of golf in an organized environment, yet before they are let out on the course, they have to sit an exam, on one of the most important, yet most neglected aspects of the game, course etiquette.

When they have passed this exam they are taken out, but at first only on the 18-hole par-3 course – again emphasizing the importance of the short game. Then there is the large practice area with its bunkered 'greens' to aim approach shots at.

And all this, let me repeat, on a *public* course. There is a message there for golf clubs, public and private, the world over!

Looking towards the green. Trying to hit such a tight green is fraught with danger and the saucer-shape adds to the difficulty unless you can place your wedge shot close to the pin.

New South Wales, Australia
Colin McGregor, Club Professional

7th hole, 408 yards

In 1768 Lieutenant James Cook of the Royal Navy set out from England in the Endeavour to chart the trail of Venus. His journey took him to the other side of the world, to the east coast of Australia where, two years later, he anchored in Botany Bay, landed and proclaimed British sovereignty over the land. A monument at Inscription Point marks the site of that historic landing. On the rocky shores of Botany Bay today, just a few miles east of Sydney, is the serene landscape of one of Australia's premier golf courses, the New South Wales.

Colin McGregor is the club's professional, one of the foremost teachers in Australian golf, and he chose for our lesson the par-4 7th, a hole that leads uphill away from the waters of the Tasman Sea, ever-present in the background.

"The wind on this hole tends to come in from left to right," he told me as we watched a group of ladies tee off.

"The wind on any seaside course is obviously a major factor, even on the green because it has far more effect on a putt than most people realise. If a putt is uphill and into the wind it can

The tee shot needs to be as long and straight as possible. The ideal spot to finish is level with or just ahead of the grassy hollow, leaving a shot of about 200 yards to the green.

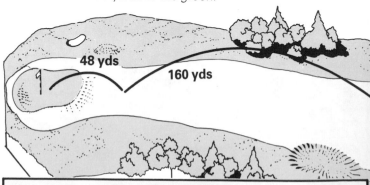

48 yds

160 yds

New South Wales
- **For a long iron shot don't have the ball too far back in your stance**
- **Make sure that you have the correct lie on your clubs**

double the 'length' of the putt. With a downhill putt with the wind behind you, you need the lightest of touches otherwise you're off the green."

However, back to the tee.

Colin is always very anxious to ensure that golfers taking lessons from him are standing correctly.

"Your arms must be hanging free, your trunk bent forward at the hips, not the knees. Then you have the space to let your arms swing through without hindrance. If you are too upright your arms have no room to swing through.

"But you must not be too stiff, even in the knees – there must be enough flexibility to swing and turn."

Golf is an athletic game despite its rather easy-going image. Although keeping fit for golf does not need the serious physical exertion required by football, for example, most rounds of golf entail a walk of four to five miles. This in itself, may be enough to keep many of us reasonably fit, but further exercises, especially to improve the flexibility of the body are beneficial.

Of course few of us either need, or want, to undertake the weight-lifting and running of a top professional like Nick Faldo to reach peak physical form. But a fit player has an extra edge, because he or she does not have to worry about tired muscles towards the end of the round, but can concentrate on their shots. Golf fitness is sometimes underestimated; a few simple stretching exercises, once the muscles are properly warmed up, can be of enormous benefit, particularly for senior players.

The tee shot here is not difficult. It needs to be as long and straight as possible, and should, from the elevated tee, reach 185 metres (200 yards) up the fairway, even though it climbs uphill. On the left of the fairway of this 376 metre (408 yards)

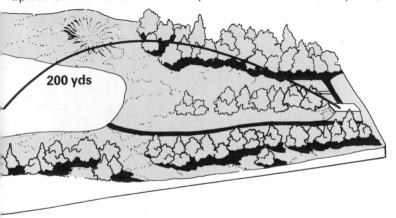

Standing correctly. Your arms should hang free, your trunk bent forward at the hips, not at the knees, allowing your arms to swing through unhindered.

hole is a grassy hollow, some 185 metres (210 yards) off the tee. Being level or just ahead of this is ideal, leaving you about the same distance.

"For a long iron shot," Colin continued, "don't have the ball too far back in your stance. The ideal spot, I think, is about three inches inside the left heel where you can hit down into the ball, pinching it out and getting both height and backspin on it.

"If you are aiming to reach the green on this shot, take the wind into account and remember what I said about putting downwind. If you are hitting into the wind, and uphill, as here, be short of the flag. If the wind is with you though, try to go past the flag to give you a more controllable putt coming back."

Very few golfers go past the flag.

"Something else that will help you hit better shots," Colin continued, "is having the correct lie on your clubs. You can test whether you have got the correct lie or not by addressing a ball on a flat surface and having a friend, or your professional, slide a coin under the toe of the club. If a coin will go under comfortably, your clubs are too upright and the heel of the club will hit the ground before the toe, closing the club-face and making you hook the ball.

"If the heel is off the ground the opposite will happen. People used to have clubs fitted perfectly – nowadays they want them off-the-shelf and quite often they don't get the correct lie. That puts them at a disadvantage even before they get out on the course."

It seems so obvious, really, yet I am sure that a check on twenty players in your local club might reveal quite a few with incorrectly fitted clubs. But back to Colin.

"If you are going to miss a green, get to know which side is the best to miss it on, even if you are short. Learn your course and get to know the parts of it that are safe."

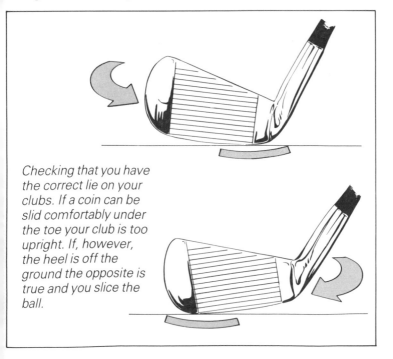

Checking that you have the correct lie on your clubs. If a coin can be slid comfortably under the toe your club is too upright. If, however, the heel is off the ground the opposite is true and you slice the ball.

Fulford, UK

Brian Hessay, Club Professional

13th hole, 473 yards

Not far from the old city of York is Fulford golf course which, for several years in the late 1980s, hosted the Benson & Hedges International Open.

Due to a potential clash with important dates on the US Tour, when many of Europe's top golfers were battling it out the other side of the Atlantic that tournament moved, in 1990, to St Mellion in Cornwall.

Past winners of the Benson & Hedges Open include Tony Jacklin, Lee Trevino, Greg Norman, Graham Marsh (twice), Sam Torrance, Sandy Lyle and Peter Baker, who beat Faldo in a play-off in 1988.

Fulford is a testing layout, as any of the professionals will testify. It is also, in some ways, an unusual design, the first and last five holes running out and back in links fashion, the middle eight running round in a loop on the other side of the York by-pass, which Bryan Hessay, the professional, and I had to cross to get to the second most difficult hole on the course, the 473-yard 13th. Unlucky for many!

The tee is very slightly elevated above the level of a fairway that is fairly flat apart from a gentle incline towards the green.

Teeing correctly is vital, because a row of gorse bushes, spectacular in their summer old gold colours, run across the

The biggest problem on the hole is the ditch that runs the entire length of the hole on the left-hand side. As the average golfer slices there is more danger for the professional who draws.

213 yds

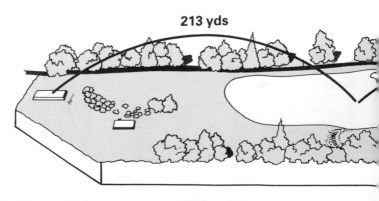

The view from the tee on the 13th at Fulford. It is advisable to tee left to avoid the gorse bushes on the right-hand side. The tee is slightly elevated above a fairly flat fairway.

front of the tee and, unless you can block them out, they could affect your thinking on how high to hit the tee shot.

The natural flight of the ball off the tee – unless you completely top it – should be more than sufficient to clear these bushes, even in mid-summer, but teeing to the left side of

Fulford

- **Play to your ability**
- **Turn your hips out of the way, particularly on a short shot**
- **Go for the middle of the green**

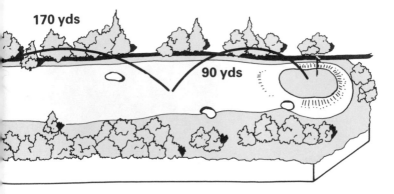

170 yds

90 yds

them, avoiding the thickest part of them, will leave you a better view of the part of the fairway that you want to hit.

"The biggest problem on this hole," Bryan told me, "and one that the professionals in particular hate, is the ditch that runs the entire length of the hole on the left side."

This natural water hazard is very close to the tee, being separated from it only by a 'collar' of semi-rough about two yards wide. The pin, on the day we played, was only seven yards from the ditch – which is not just a hazard but also, more dangerously, out-of-bounds. The ditch is very deep too.

The professionals, Bryan explained, like to hit their shots with draw, getting extra yardage out of a ball that travels through the air right-to-left.

"The average club golfer, however," Bryan explained, "often hits the ball with some slice. Here, that would be the better shot – or at least the safer."

Apart from avoiding the left, the first other obstacle to drive around is the bunker on the left, at 243 yards off the back of the tee. We were actually playing from a slightly forward position, 15 yards on, so that bunker came into play at just over 225 yards – an average sort of drive.

"I would suggest you take a 3-wood to be certain of being just short of that bunker," Bryan said. "There is another reason,

The second shot. It is important to work out where you want this to land. A shot finishing between the bunkers leaves an easy 9-iron to the green.

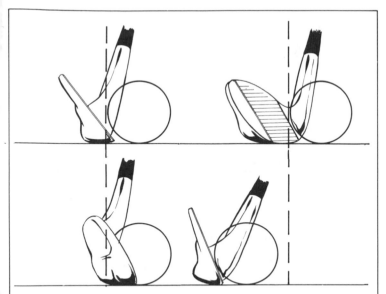

Hooding and closing the face. (Top left) The face is square on. (Top right) The face is open.(Bottom left) The face is closed. (Bottom right) The face is hooded. Turn the face over slightly but still pointing squarely at the target.

too. It would be virtually impossible for you to reach the green in two. A professional might be able to hit a drive 273 yards then an iron 200 yards – few club players, even with a good tail-wind, would do that. You need to look at it as a par-5. It has an index of two, so you get an extra stroke.''

"You have to look at the second and third shots. Assuming that you need three to reach the green you should work out where you want the second shot to land.''

A look at the course planner showed bunkers either side of the fairway, at 125 yards and 87 yards from the green.

"A shot placed between these bunkers is ideal, leaving you a 9-iron onto the green,'' Bryan told me.

A 5-iron for the second shot – the 3-wood having landed at 200 yards, leaving 260 yards to the green – was pushed forward 160 yards without too much effort, clearing the first bunker easily and coming up short of the second. This really was 'thinking golf' for there was no way to reach the green, and hitting as far as possible with that second shot could have put the ball into difficulties.

From here a 100-yard 9-iron was sufficient, and, with a fairly strong left-to-right wind, a slight uphill incline to the green, and

The ditch that runs the length of the left-hand side of the hole really is a hazard. The second shot should therefore be played towards the middle of the green.

the green being very narrow, a low shot was better than a real up-and-under.

"You must go for the middle of the green," Bryan told me, "to avoid the bunker on the right and the ditch on the left. Play the ball off the back foot with the face hooded. Turn the face over slightly but still with the face pointing squarely at the target. Don't confuse hooding with closing.

"It is important to come through this shot well, turning your hips out of the way to give enough room to swing through. Too many people fail to clear their hips out of the way, and end up blocking the shot right.

"You must ensure that your hips rotate and don't just sway left, giving enough room for your arms and the clubhead to come through to impact and into the follow-through, with your body turned at the target. That turn, on approach shots like this (100 yards), really is vital. Many players think that, because it is such a short shot, they don't need to turn. They end up pushing the ball out right."

Fortunately, my approach did not miss the green, and a two-putt secured a five, with the stroke index of two, good enough for a net par.

That really is the only way to play this hole. Attempting a four, at least to reach the green in two, is just not an option open to most golfers.

The Belfry, UK

18th hole, 455 yards

So we come, almost, to the end of this book and the final test of what we have learnt. This series of par-4 holes has taken us across the world, to Australia, the United States, and across Europe, from Stockholm in the far north to the Adriatic coast of Italy, from Costa del Sol to St Andrews and then, one of the finest par-4s in the world, the infamous Road Hole.

But now here we are at the last hole and there is no tougher finishing hole in the world of golf than the final hole on the Brabazon Course of The Belfry.

This was of course the venue of the 1985 and 1989 Ryder Cup matches between Europe and the United States. Few who watched either of those epic struggles can ever forget the magnificent shot across the water by Sam Torrance in 1985 to claim the Cup for Britain and Europe; nor Christy O'Connor Jnr's immaculate 2-iron to the green on the last day to claim the Cup again for the home side in 1989.

Playing that eighteenth hole, and our eighteenth, is the most fitting challenge with which to conclude this book.

The hole measures 455 yards off the medal tee – the Ryder Cup players and professionals in the other tournaments held at the Belfry move back slightly to make it 474 yards. It remains,

The tee shot on the difficult 18th hole at The Belfry, has to be hit across water and carry the first part of the lake. It is a matter of courage how far left you go.

therefore, a par-4, though just another three feet would turn it into a par-5.

The hole dog-legs left with the tee shot having to be hit across water, then the second shot, or perhaps third, across the lake again to the green which slopes from back to front. Many 1989 Ryder Cup players found the lake with their second shots, including several Americans, Seve Ballesteros and Nick Faldo.

For us mere mortals, no Christy O'Connor type heroics are called for; safety should be the key to this hole. I teed up, back on the medal tee, in ideal golfing conditions – warm, with little wind, and the sun just beginning to break through.

The tee shot must carry the first part of the lake, going as far left as you dare. From the tee a shot hit perfectly straight must carry about 190 yards to clear the lake, though anything over 200 will put you in a good position for the second shot.

Getting to the tee the first thing to do was to follow the excellent advice of Linwood Taylor, from Tanglewood in North Carolina, who had told us to look carefully not so much at the par figure for the hole, but the stroke index.

Here at The Belfry the par is a four, but the stroke index is six, meaning that most of us receive a welcome stroke on this testing hole.

Ray Leach, from Toxandria in Holland, had also suggested some good advice – relax. I took a few practice swings, with a graphite shafted metal 3-wood, as used by Tommy Horton from Royal Jersey, and remembered the advice of his fellow Channel-Islander, David Melville: "Understand how to play a course – don't just hit and hope!"

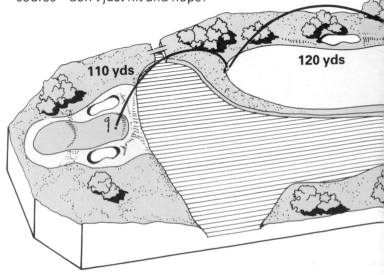

My aim here was to play this as an easy par-5, using the stroke that the index gave. Obviously with the two areas of water to carry, on both the tee shot and the approach, and looking carefully at the plan of the hole, it was apparent that the chances of hitting a long tee-shot, then a long iron over the water, safely, were fairly remote.

The plan, then, was to play it as a par-5, putting the tee shot in play safely across the lake, then laying-up before chipping across to the green and, hopefully, two-putting for a net par.

Preparing for the tee shot the most important aspects are, as Ian Marchbank from that wonderful Gleneagles course said, "eighty per cent before you reach the ball". The set-up, grip, stance and backswing are all vital, with the back of the left hand pointing towards the target across the lake, feet and body standing square to that target and the takeaway smooth and low.

The tee shot landed across the lake, safely, at a point opposite the first bunker, with exactly 215 yards to go to the front of the green, a further fifteen to the flag.

I was tempted to decide what I was going to do before I reached the ball but recalled the words of Peter Tupling when we played the Road Hole at St Andrews: "Never decide which club you are going to use before you reach the ball."

On looking at the ball, and checking again the distances, it was clear that a shot across the water, though spectacular if it worked, was not a serious possibility. Christy O'Connor Jnr might have managed it – but not me.

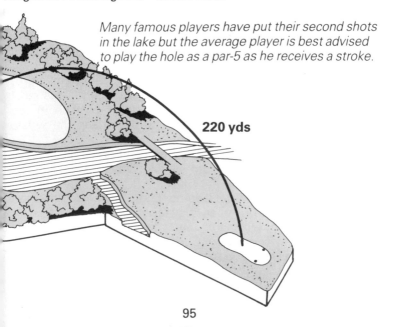

Many famous players have put their second shots in the lake but the average player is best advised to play the hole as a par-5 as he receives a stroke.

220 yds

The third shot from a fluffy lie after laying-up just before the lake. The distance to the front of the green is 100 yards. In the background is the club-house.

A 9-iron to lay-up before the lake was the sensible choice. As Charlotte Montgomery from Drottningholm had suggested: "If you are going to lay-up leave yourself with at least a three-quarter shot."

I pushed it slightly to the right, where it gave the shortest route across the lake, the ball just rolling off into the very light rough, giving a fluffy lie for the approach. The distance of the second shot was 115 yards, leaving 100 yards to the front of the green.

The first two shots had gone where I wanted them – the third, an approach across the water to the lake, was slightly pushed. I had failed to do what Bob McCavery from Lahinch in the Emerald Isle had tried to impress on me: "Keep the wrists loose, flexible, on the approach shots."

My ball did, however, land on the green, towards the right front edge, some 13 yards from the flag, leaving an uphill putt that would break right to left.

I aimed above the hole, let it come round and the ball stopped a foot from the pin, leaving an easy tap-in for a five, net four.

By playing the hole sensibly and safely, with no heroics, no imitations of Sam Torrance or Christy O'Connor, the result was as satisfactory as could be expected.

The splendid advice from all our professionals, quite simply, really does work.